VOICES:

AN ANNOTATED ANTHOLOGY OF CONTEMPORARY BAHRAINI POETRY

Translated and Edited by

Hasan Marhamah

Introduction by

Alawi Al-Hashmi

Order this book online at www.trafford.com
or email orders@trafford.com

Most Trafford titles are also available at major online book retailers.

Printed in Victoria, BC, Canada.

ISBN: 978-1-4269-1684-7 (sc)

Our mission is to efficiently provide the world's finest, most comprehensive book publishing service, enabling every author to experience success. To find out how to publish your book, your way, and have it available worldwide, visit us online at www.trafford.com

Trafford rev. 01/29/2010

www.trafford.com

North America & international
toll-free: 1 888 232 4444 (USA & Canada)
phone: 250 383 6864 • fax: 812 355 4082

Acknowledgement

My thanks and gratitude are due to all friends, colleagues and dear ones: without their constant support and encouragement, this anthology would not have been accomplished.

For My children: Mustafa, Murtadha & Maysa

Contents

Preface

From the outset, I would like to draw the reader's attention to the fact that translation is one of the most complex and controversial disciplines today. Throughout history, there were two distinct tendencies in translating texts and in particular literary texts. The first method binds the translator to capturing the author's spirit and feelings and transferring them honestly to the translated text. In other words, concentration is focused more or less on content rather than form. The second method, on the other hand, requires that the translator should conform to the form or the structure of the text, its linguistic components, musical devices, and rhyme and rhythm.

I am of opinion that both methods lack a major component: the reader and his role in understanding the translated text. Obviously, the translated text will be of a limited value or valueless if the reader finds it unintelligible or unexciting. Apparently, the attempt to distance the reader from the centre to the margin of the text is not confined to translation but to all literary writings.

If we take these three issues: the content, the form and the reader into consideration, can we then obtain a compatible translated text? Interestingly enough, the ancient Greek philosophers used the term 'imitation' but not compatibility, mainly because it is impossible to find two seemingly similar or compatible things in nature. Hence, how and why do we search for two compatible texts?

It can be claimed, therefore, that what a translator aims at is not to obtain similarity or compatibility with the original text. Furthermore, the modifications or deletions that occur to the translated text are necessities of translation. In short, a literary text in the translation process is like the Phoenix: it must pass through the stages of death and life. In other words, a text dies in order to let another text survive which will have a different feature, a distinct power, and this stage is both detrimental and inevitable.

Thus, if we assume that a poetic text is distinguished from other literary texts from the point of view of poetic experience, imagery, rhythm, metre and language, which often includes structures based on poetic license, it is therefore valid to state that a translated poetic text may lack artistic and poetic elements. Having said so, this of course does not mean that poetic texts should not be translated into prose: in the most difficult cases, a translator prefers prose, especially if the original poetic text contains poetic restrictions which cannot be rendered into prose.

Earlier we referred to a third component to any translation process and that is the reader. In this connection, we are concerned mostly with readers who are English-speaking whose mother-tongue is English or near-English. After the Second World War, there emerged in most English-speaking countries such as Britain and the USA, or in countries where English was a second language such as India, or Nigeria, new themes in poetry, which basically focused on daily subjects, mystical revelations and reflections, and everyday affairs. [**1**] Apart from one or two militant voices from Wales, Scotland or Ireland, [**2**] English poetry since the Second World War, became a platform for unpatriotic, un-political and un-social subjects.

Can a contemporary Bahraini poet fulfil the aesthetic needs of the English-speaking readers of this century? Can English-speaking readers in Britain, Ireland, Australia, New Zealand, America and the sub-Indian/African continents digest the deep meanings of translated Bahraini poetry which is characterized by two distinct qualities: subjectivity and political commitment?

As will be mentioned in the Introduction, the fourth wave of Bahraini poets, the Neo-Realists, lived in a period which was rightly called the 'Henderson era'. [**3**] Tens of young Bahraini intellectuals were arrested and imprisoned under the pretext of being 'leftists' or communists'. Such operations were administered and supervised by Ian Henderson who was the head of Intelligence in Bahrain. The whole country was haunted by 'The Henderson ghost'. [**4**] Furthermore, this period also witnessed the widespread influence of modern Arabic poetry especially the poetry of the Iraqi, Badr Shakir Al-Sayaab, the Egyptian Ahmad Hejazi, the Palestinian Mahmud Darwish and the Syrian Adonis. [**5**]

The impact of these poets, in particular on language and imagery of young Bahraini poets, was indelible. It is, therefore, the explicit political pronouncements coupled with the complexity of Adonis' language that produced the contemporary Bahraini poetry of the sixties, and seventies. Furthermore, the Eliotian concept of 'Objective Correlation' aptly applies in this context. The political events of the sixties provided Bahraini readers with a sense of correlation; they could understand the historical and political background to these poems. The texts never alienated them: on the contrary, they provided them with a platform on which they could respond and identify with the events. However, the poets who began to write in the eighties and the years after, encountered certain unprecedented political events. First, there was the Islamic Revolution in Iran in 1979, and its propelling impact on the younger poets. Marxist fervour was gradually substituted by a more militant Islamic enthusiasm. Conducive to that was the collapse of the Soviet Union and its Socialist system in 1991.

What made the political milieu in Bahrain more stable and to some extent restrained, was the king's democratic reforms which eventually put an end to oppressive means of harassment and imprisonment. [**6**]

Hence, a look at the poems written by the younger poets, during or in the post-democracy era, will exhibit a totally different picture: there is a lack of symmetry and sensibility at both the linguistic and poetic levels, which thwarts the ability of the voice to pronounce itself outside the text. Furthermore, readers are presented with an amalgam of surrealist images woven into far-fetched and complex figures of speech. The political and social flavour is there, but often imbued with a series of entwined images. Nevertheless, these are the natural and inevitable voices that reflect the true and sober feelings of the younger poets in Bahrain.

As mentioned earlier, the translated poetic text in the process of translation is transferred to a next text as a result of additions and deletions. This new text has its own characteristics. These changes will naturally apply to the translated Bahraini poetry. [7]

Undoubtedly, there are some difficulties facing a translator of contemporary Bahraini poetry into English. These difficulties are general and they should not hinder the translation process. Some of these difficulties are linguistic, some cultural, and some semiotic. [**8**]

I have endeavoured in this translation to adhere as much as possible to the original text by rendering the poems into standard English, avoiding clichés, and or the use of colloquial words or phrases. I have also tried my best to enhance the translated poems with some aesthetic value in form and content that may appeal to English-speaking readers. Obviously, my intended readers, in this regard, are not Arabic-speaking readers, though they are welcome to enjoy reading the book. The extensive historical, political and religious notes and explanations added to the Introduction and the poems are meant to provide English-speaking readers with necessary information about various aspects of life in Bahrain in connection with the development of poetry in the region.

In this annotated anthology, I have selected poems from different phases of this century, starting with the father of Modern Bahraini Poetry, Ibrahim Al-Arrayedh. I have also included most of the poets mentioned by Dr. Alawi Al-Hashmi in his book '*Contemporary Poets of Bahrain*'. A large selection of Bahraini women poets and poems from the younger generation have also been included in this anthology. My sincere apology goes out to those Bahraini poets whose names were left out because of the inaccessibility of their poems or their biographies. The anthology is not, therefore, comprehensive of all contemporary Bahraini poets.

The poets are arranged in chronological order irrespective of fame or publication date. However, in the Biographical Notes, the arrangement of the poets is based on alphabetical order. Last but not least, I take personal responsibility for any inaccuracy in translation, linguistic errors or any misrepresentation of information in this anthology.

Notes:

1. The era of W.H. Auden and his socialist friends MacNeice, Lewis and Spender is over in Britain: instead we hear the voices of more conservative poets, such as Tony Harrison, Hugo Williams, James Fenton. Martin Booth (1985) describes British poetry as "a mess: it has lost itself in a bog of indifference, apathy and artlessness such as it has never seen before." According to Blake Morrison and Andrew Motion (1982) "...British poetry is once again undergoing a transition" and in *The Penguin Book of Contemporary British Poetry* (1982), the names of the masters of modern English poetry such as Ted Hughes, Geoffrey Hill, Philip Larkin, Donald Davie, Charles Tomlinson, and Thom Gunn, are excluded.

2. I refer in particular to the poetry of the Rev. Ronald Stuart Thomas (1913-2000). His anti-English political poems are often fused with references to Welsh history and literary heritage. However, R.S. Thomas, in his later poems, resorted to more philosophical and mystical tendencies. The Irish Nobel prize winner, Seamus Heaney (1939-), was not as daring as Thomas in his politics, yet his *Bog poems* clearly touched upon the "experience of the contemporary Irish Troubles."

3. Colonel Ian Henderson (1928-) was a British citizen who was dispatched first to Kenya to quell the uprising there. Later on, he was appointed Head of Intelligence Services in Bahrain. During thirty years or more in Bahrain, Henderson committed the most inhumane and ruthless acts against the Bahraini intellectuals. Thousands of young men and women were arrested, tortured, imprisoned and eventually murdered or exiled. The BBC Home affairs analyst, Jon Silverman, reporting on Wednesday, 16 April, 2003, stated that, according to "organizations such as Human Rights Watch and Amnesty, the methods used to cow anti-government activists included beatings, sexual abuse and the ransacking of whole villages."

4. A political allusion describing the politics of the 'communist hunt' which was propagated by Senator Joseph McCarthy in the forties and fifties in the United Sates. Thousands of American citizens including academics, writers and singers were arrested for being communist sympathizers. Arthur Miller's *The Crucible* is a true representation of the atrocities of the McCarthy era.

5. The most flourishing period in the history of Arabic poetry began in the mid twentieth century as a reaction against the Romantic trend of the age. Most of the poets who raised the banner of innovations and commitment were Marxist or Socialist in ideology. It began initially with the critical writings of Egyptian socialists such as Salama Moosa, Lewis Awad and Abdul Rahman Sharqawi. Gradually the call for a new poetry was spread in the Arab world. In Iraq, it was immediately embraced by Badr Shakir Al-Sayaab, Abdul Wahab Al-Bayati, Buland Al-Haideri and Nazek Al-

Malaeka; in Egypt and the Sudan by Ahmad Hejazi, Salah Abdul Saboor, Mohammd Faituri, Taj al-Sirr Hasan, Jili Abdul Rahman; in Syria and Lebanon by Hawi, Al-Khal, Adonis, Nezar Qabbani and in Palestine by Mahmud Darwish, Samih Al-Qasim, and Tawfiq Zeyaad. One source of influence on these poets was, undoubtedly, the burst and acceleration of Socialist ideals and views around the world, the second, amazingly enough, was the effects of T.S. Eliot's poetry and his critical theories.

6. The late Amir, Sheikh Isa Bin Salman Al-Khalifa ruled Bahrain from 1961 to 1999. In 1973, The National Assembly was held but it was dissolved in 1975. After his demise in 1999, his son Sheikh Hamad Bin Isa Al-Khalifa ascended the throne. His reign was marked by a series of reforms. A Consultative Council was set up to replace the old National Assembly. In 2001, Bahrain became a constitutional monarchy. The notorious state security law was abolished: all exiled political prisoners and detainees were released and returned home and political societies and women's organizations were made legal.

7. In addition to the linguistic competence that a translator should possess in both languages, there is also another hindrance a translator must overcome: the flavour of the original text. The intention here is not to indicate that Bahraini Gulf poet does not use standard Arabic or uses one of the Arabic dialects; the essence of the subject here is that a Bahraini Gulf poet injects into his language a special flavour and this special linguistic flavour must be taken heed of by the translator. Special care must be given to the rendering of local and indigenous terms some of which do not have equivalents in English. Unfortunately, any attempt by the translator to delete or avoid these terms will result in a misunderstanding of the main idea of the poem. A thorough understanding of Bahraini Gulf culture, traditions and values will naturally help in transferring the bulk of the idea to the translated text.

8. The significance of semiotics, in particular cultural semiotics in translating literary texts is already an established fact. It is the signified aspect of the word rather than its signifier that carries diverse meanings. Words such as the sea, palm-tree, a pearl are more than connotations or even symbols; these are signs whose signifiers are deeply rooted in the culture of Bahraini society.

Introduction*

It is generally agreed upon today that the Arabian Peninsula was the fountainhead of the first wave of Arabic poetry; indeed there is historical evidence according to Dr. Ihsan Abbas to assume that "poetry in the Eastern Province was more advanced in years than in other parts of the Arabian Peninsula." [**1**]

It was in the Eastern Province that the first seeds of Arabic poetry were planted and the voices of the forerunners of Arabic poetry such as Al-Muhalal, Al-Mutlamas, Al-Muthqab, Amru Bin Qumeina and Tarfa and his sister Al-Kharnaq and the Great and Small Marqashan were heard. These poets enjoyed the best part of their life on the banks of the Eastern Province of the Arabian Peninsula and played a vital role in reviving the Arabic literary movement in particular poetry. Hence, many cultural aspects, poetic elements, and profound psychological images were added to Arabic poetry are attributed to them.

Furthermore, the Province was swarmed with renowned Arab literary markets such as (Dareen and Al-Jarha and Al-Zaarah, Hajer and Oman, Al_Mashqar Dubai and Suhar). [**2**] Many delegations from all over the Arabian Peninsula joined and participated in these gatherings by reciting poetry, delivering eloquent speeches, signing treaties and alliances and setting up artistic carnivals. These early poetic threads remained in tact and united throughout various periods of the Islamic State, in particular in the Abbasid's and Omayyad's rule. [**3**]

However, this stability ceased when eventually the region became a fertile ground for the insurgents and the rebels who rose against the central authority of the Islamic State and also the refugees who fled the country.

Moreover, the region became a centre for successive rebellions such as Al-khwarij, [**4**[Al-Qaramita [**5**] and Al-Zinj. [**6**] This turbulent political situation influenced the experience of poets and their poetry. It imbued their themes with special contextual elements which made their poetry belong to one clique, either with the warriors or the dogmatists.

Several poets of the region rose to fame during the Abbasid period, but the climax of the poetic flourishing of the Age according to Abdulla Al-Mubarak was represented by a master poet: Ibn Al-Muqarrab Al-Uyuni (1176-1231). [7] He was the descendant of the Al-Uynid dynasty [**8**] which ended the reign of Al-Qaramita. There are several other poets who established their fame during the sixteenth and seventeenth centuries, the most famous and notable ones were Bin Sulayman Al-Nabhan, and Jafar Al-Khati, who lived between Qatif, his birth place, and Bahrain, where he composed one of his most well-known poems called "Al-Sabitiyaya".

After these two poets (Al-Nabhan and Al-khati), there emerged another group of poets, as mentioned by Abdulla Al-Mubarak, the last and the most prominent of whom was Sayed Abdul Jalil Al-Tabatabai (1776-1853). He was born in Al-Basra and moved between El-Ehssa, Qatar, Bahrain and Kuwait. His role in invigorating the cultural ambience and the literary and poetic movements in the Gulf region and the Arabian Peninsula is well recorded. This could be attributed to his frequent movement in the region between Al-Basra, Kuwait, El-Ehssa, Zubara, Bahrain and Al-Hejaz.

Al-Tabatabai conducted poetry contests with the literary personalities of the countries he stayed in or passed through. This was, indeed, a prelude to a new poetry revival movement which prevailed throughout the region after some years. It was also an exemplary picture of a poet and a writer like Al Tabatabai, who through his manners and poems, embodied the integration and unity of the region before it was divided into political and scattered territories by the colonialists.

The debate about the actual location of poets such as Al-Tabatabai and their descent from one territory began after the region was divided into small territories. The geographical location of these poets, and their displacement from one region to another, is a controversial issue in academic research studies even at the present time. These poets were once confined geographically to one of the territories of the Great Bahrain Region [**9**] prior to the arrival of Neo-Colonialism.

Nevertheless, since the inception of the modern literary renaissance in Bahrain, there have been outstanding and distinctive achievements in poetry, even recently. The poetic scene has moved through bright phases of intellectual development. This can be recorded and divided into four phases according to their chronological order. Hence, the following descriptions may be applied to these four phases:

1- The Classical Movement

2- The Neo-Classical Movement

3- The Romantic Movement

4- The Neo-Realist and Modernist Movement

Most poets of the Classical and Neo-Classical Movements who followed both trends, the traditional and modern, however, had already deceased, albeit their biographies and poems could be traced in various literary and history books. Therefore, they will receive a special translation and documentation section in this condensed essay. The poets of the last two movements, the Romantics and Neo-Realists, on the other hand, will be presented through an analytical and critical appreciation.

1-The Classical Movement

Although the advent of the Classical Movement in the Gulf region and the Arabian Peninsula was somewhat slow, its effect on Bahraini poets, however, was substantial to the extent that it was influenced more than other countries in the region. This was due to the growth in the crucial structures of modern life in Bahrain such as clubs (1913), education (1919) journalism and health clinics (1939).

Furthermore, the nationalist movement which was led by Sheikh Abdul Wahab Al-Zayani and his comrades against colonialism reached its zenith in 1923. [**10**]

At the head list of this Movement, there emerged a group of poets with a thoroughly traditional outlook. Their work was prevalent from the late nineteenth century to the first decade of the twentieth century.

This group was led by Sheikh Ibrahim Bin Mohammad Al-Khalifa, Sheikh Salman Al-Tajer (Al Nashra) and Sheikh Mohammad Bin Isa Al-Khalifa. The traditional features in their poetry can be traced in their use of themes such as self-praise, panegyric, courtship and lament on the passing of time, and nostalgia for the past. Their poetry was characterized by a purity of style, a firmness of language and a manipulation of resonant phrases fused with intensive patriotic tone, especially in their nationalistic poems, which were the outcome of their last poetic phase.

The prince poet Sheikh Ibrahim Bin Mohammad Al-Khalifa was born in the city of Al-Muharraq in 1850. His father was Sheikh Mohammad Bin Khalifa who ruled Bahrain in sporadic periods before the reign of his cousin Sheikh Isa Bin Ali. In literary terms, the poet's literary experience embodied a solid classical foundation on which the revival of contemporary Bahraini poetry was based. Keen on the use of direct solemn expressions, Sheikh Ibrahim rarely resorted to daring imagery, figures of speech or musical devices. Furthermore, his extensive experience in writing and reciting Nabatean poetry [**11**] left a potent effect on his later poetry in classical standard Arabic.

Sheikh Salman Al-Tajer was born in the city of Manamah in 1875 and he represents, together with Sheikh Ibrahim Bin Mohammad Al-Khalifa, the cornerstone of the school of revival in Bahrain and in the Arabian Peninsula at both poetic and cultural levels. Al-Tajer's poetic experience was known to have focused on religious occasions. However, the poet often seemed to have adopted such events as a platform for his calls for reforms and for learning messages seeking awakening. Sheikh Salman Al-Tajer was also known for his rigorous imitation of the style of classical Arabic poetry. [**12**[

Sheikh Mohammad Bin Isa Al-Khalifa was born in 1876, ten years after the rule of his father, Isa Bin Ali in Bahrain. The poet did not receive any formal education but relied basically on traditional learning which was available at that time. Such dispositions included: reading the Holy Quran, attending his father's court, travelling to many Arab and European countries, his vast knowledge of the traditional literary heritage and meeting with personalities and his correspondence with writers inside and outside Bahrain. The poet lived long enough to witness the most important events in Bahrain and to experience them in modern life. He began writing Nabatean poems, as stated by Abdullah Al-Tai, but because of his travels to Arab countries such as Syria, Iraq, Egypt and Saudi Arabia, the poet was eventually encouraged to compose classical Arabic poetry. His successful composition of classical poetry continued up to the end of his life to the extent that he began to persuade other Nabatean poets to write classical Arabic poetry.

2-The Neo-Classical Movement

This trend is considered a continuation of the first Classical Movement in poetry. Most of its prominent poets were the disciples of Sheikh Ibrahim Al-Khalifa, and Sheikh Salman Al-Tajer. Furthermore, they were regular attendants of their masters' private gatherings and the literary club which the two Sheikhs helped to establish in 1920. The aim of this literary club was to welcome and honour Arab literary personalities by the two masters and their prospective followers, such as Abdulla Al-Zayed, Abdul Rahman Al-Moawda and Qasim Al-Shirawi. The poets of this phase were greatly influenced by the Classical poets.

Most literary and intellectual characteristics of their poetry focused on a call for reforms, education and nationalist awareness. Obviously, the genesis of such a tendency had already taken place in the Classical Movement but it blossomed and was cherished in the poetic work of the Neo-Classical poets.

The nationalist uprising which emerged in 1923, beginning with Sheikh Abdul Wahab Al-Zayani, had a direct bearing on exploding those poetic themes which were embedded in classical poetry. Subsequently, they prospered to become salient and conspicuous literary features of the Neo-Classical Movement. Ahmad Al-Manai in *An Introduction to Modern Literary Movements in Bahrain* presents this movement as 'a trend which used national and religious occasions to call for social reforms'.

At the head of this Movement, were Abdulla Al-Zayed and Abdul Rahman Al-Moawdah from Bahrain, and Abdul Aziz Al-Rasheed and Khalid Al-Faraj from Kuwait. In their poetry, there is a note of yearning for the past expressed in a dejected spirit and grieved outlook. They glorify the warriors of the past and manipulate their deeds as poetic themes to excite people and provoke their feelings and enthusiasm.

Sheikh Qasim Mohammad Al-Shirawi who was born in 1880 and died in 1950, represents an essential linking-point, at both intellectual and nationalist levels, between the Classical and Neo-Classical Movements. Despite the fact that there is insufficient information about the poet, yet, his news and poems, the positions that he held, his companionship with Abdulla Al-Zayed and his close relationship with Sheikh Ibrahim, are enough evidence to affirm his influential part in the intellectual and political life of Bahrain in the first four decades of the twentieth century.

Abdulla Bin Ali Jabar Al-Zayed was born in the city of Al-Muharraq. Al-Zayed was descended from a well-known Arab family in Bahrain and the Arabian Gulf as stated by the critic Mubarak Al-Khater. His father was a famous pearl merchant in Bahrain. Al-Zayed read and memorized the Holy Quran in four months. [**13**] He also attended the private classes of one of the prominent teachers of Arabic language and Jurisprudence. Later, and as advised by his master Sheikh Ibrahim Bin Mohammad Al-Khalifa, he joined a private local school administered by Mr. Mohammad Saleh Yousif.

Al-Zayed followed his father's profession as a pearl merchant. [**14**] However, he later encountered the worst personal tragedy that affected his life. Al-Zayed was accused of dealing with fake pearls and, consequently, was exiled to Bombay in India for two years. While in exile, Al-Zayed visited many European countries, such as Italy, France, and Britain. After staying one year in London, Al-Zayed came home. One of the positive outcomes of his exile and travels was his acquaintance with various aspects of modern life and culture and his enthusiasm for science, knowledge and reforms. In 1934, Al-Zayed was able to procure the first modern printing machine in Bahrain and to launch the first Arabic journal (Al-Bahrain) which was meant to be the basis for modern culture in Bahrain and the Gulf region.

The publication of the first edition of Al-Bahrain coincided with the circumstances of the Second World War. The British, though supporting Al-Zayed in his venture, nevertheless, committed a most unjust act of exploitation by using the journal for their own political propaganda. [**15**] This was seen by some as an act of collaboration with the colonialists. Al-Zayed's reputation was again blemished: some tried to stab at his patriotism and his true intellectual, social and political leanings at that critical time of nationalist awakening. These two events, concerning the pearls and the journal, left a great and deep psychological impact on Al-Zayed. He expressed his agony in a sad poem that he wrote months before his death, in which he lamented his fate in the following lines:

'Wearied with life and long vigil

I longed for death and the grave as my residence

For in death misfortunes are at a distance

If Time betrays or proves brutal.'

The poetic experience of both poets Abdul Rahman Al-Moawdah and Sayed Redhi Al-Mosawi embodies the climax of this Neo-Classical period. They are the last two names on the list before the Movement synchronized and intersected eventually with the Romantic Movement, which was strongly represented by the well-known poet, Ibrahim Al-Arrayedh and his disciples, Ahmad Mohammad Al-Khalifa, Gazi Al-Gosaibi and Abdul Rahman Rafi. Moreover, a large portion of the experience of both Al-Moawdah and Al-Mosawi illustrates aspects of strong Romantic tendencies, on the part of each poet, which caused some difficulties at all levels.

The poet Abdul Rahman Al-Moawdah, who was born in the city of Al-Muharraq in 1911, underwent a unique poetic and nationalist experience in Bahrain.

Such a distinct quality consolidated the inseparable bond and organic relation between his poetry and the political reality in Bahrain. Consequently, this ushered in the birth of poetic drama which Al-Moawdah mastered and in which he wrote more than ten poetic plays. These plays were performed for ten years on the stage of private schools that Al-Moawdah established in mid thirties and forties.

The poet Sayed Redhi Al-Mosawi, on the other hand, was born in 1916 into a conservative and religious family. His early poetic writings displayed the influence of traditional trends in form and content. However, his transfer to the city of Manamah, unveiled new prospects for knowledge and paved the way for his meeting with the master poet Ibrahim Al-Arrayedh. One of the most fruitful results that Al-Mosawi gained in the city, was his acquiring a wide ranging culture and his exposure to the contemporary life and the harsh realities of people in society. Nationalist and patriotic issues prevailed in most of his poems. This eventually led to the traditional tendency, which was represented in his religious poems, fading away. Hence, Al-Mosawi successfully emerged from the poetic cocoon that the majority of religious poets in Bahrain had failed to do.

3- The Romantic Movement

The Romantic Movement in Arabic literature, [**16**] as it is known with all its characteristics, is considered a revolution from Classical Arabic poetry in two major aspects: tradition and reinvention. Therefore, these two movements emerged as two synchronized and intersected entities with similar features in Bahraini poetry since the publication of the first volume of poetry by the master poet Ibrahim Al- Arrayedh in 1931. It contained a critical preface which was seen as the manifesto for the Romantic Movement in Bahrain and the Arabian Gulf.

For this reason, Al-Arrayedh is considered the founding father of Romanticism in the Gulf region, though some critics regarded the Kuwaiti poet Fahad Al-Askar [**17**] as the mentor. Nevertheless, early theoretical formation and extensive literary production, from both intellectual and poetical perspectives, make Al-Arrayedh indisputably the pioneer of this movement. However, Fahad Al-Askar may have displayed, in his poetic experience, literary characteristics of Romanticism.

Although traces of Romanticism can be noted in the Neo-Classical Movement, in particular in the poetry of Al-Waeli, Al-Moawdah and Al-Mosawi, nevertheless, Romanticism, as a strong and fertile tendency, emerged with Al-Arrayedh's experience. It was in the beginning of the third decade of the last century that Al-Arrayedh returned home from

India and began the publication of a great number of poetry collections and literary, critical and translated books. [**18**]

He, therefore, paved the way for a wider manipulation of Romantic theories which were taken up by a number of poets led by Sheikh Ahmad Al-Khalifa, Gazi Al-Gosaibi and Abdul Rahman Rafi. The younger poets who came after and were known as Neo-Romantic poets or the transitional poets of the Neo-Realist Movement in poetry behaved similarly, as we shall see.

The essential principle on which the Romantic Movement in Bahraini poetry was based since its rise, even before Ibrahim Al-Arrayedh, was its rally around poetic subjectivity and the poet's individualism which obviously affected the poetic elements of poetry. This will explain the theoretical and critical efforts undertaken by Ibrahim Al-Arrayedh in this regard, even in his early poetic experience.

Furthermore, his concern with the themes of women and nature were to be seen as the features of his romantic experience. Likewise, we should consider the themes of homeland and mankind, which are all together considered the pillars of contemporary poetry in Bahrain.

Nevertheless, the Romantic idiosyncrasy of indifference in internal matters and the escape from the involvement in political and realist issues, did not prevent the romantic poets in Bahrain, led by Ibrahim Al-Arrayedh, from expressing their concern about the Arab and humanitarian causes which were broader and more universal than those of homeland issues. According to the critic Mohammad Jabber Al-Ansari, there were two perspectives in the poetic movement in Bahrain: local and Arab. Al-Ansari considered Ibrahim Al-Arrayedh, a good example of those poets who addressed Arab readers in general. The second trend was concerned with the people's suffering and distress and this was represented by Al-Zayed's comrades such as Abdul Rahman Al-Moawdah, Qasim Al-Shirawi and Redhi Al-Mosawi.

The poetic career of the transitional poet Ahmad Mohammad Al-Khalifa constitutes a contact point between the Romantic-Realist experience of Ibrahim Al-Arrayedh on the one hand, and the liberal Romanticism of Gazi Al-Gosaibi [**19**] and Abdul Rahman Rafi. [**20**]

The poet Ahmad Mohammad Al-Khalifa was not only influenced by Al-Arrayedh but his poetic experience and in particular his first volume, *Songs from Bahrain*, which contained sentimental patriotic and descriptive poems, displayed a strong affinity with the poetry of the two Arab poets, Ali Mahmoud Taha and Omar Abu Reesha. [**21**]

Hence, he took part in Arab heroic events of the fifties and whole-heartedly lived with them in his poetry. His glorifying of the Egyptian, Moroccan and Algerian Revolutions, and his songs to Palestine, are remarkable examples of his nationalist tendencies. Furthermore, the local milieu and in particular the general surroundings, had a noticeable place in the poetry of Ahmad Mohammad Al-Khalifa, as mentioned by Abdullah Al-Tai in his book *Contemporary Literature in the Arabian Gulf.* He is, therefore, one of the early poets in Bahrain who attended to the aspects of diving or the diver's experience which were later developed by Ali Abdulla Khalifa, albeit, that the poet did not touch on the sufferings of the divers as Ali Abdulla Khalifa did. Moreover, the poet's treatment of the subject-matter of diving was descriptive and motivated by a sense of pride and with the purpose of eulogy.

Apparently, the Romantic Movement failed to go beyond the complications of dualism in Romantic theories, one of which being the confinement of the poet's self from expressing broader Arab and international realist issues. However, a small number of Neo-Romantic poets whose poetic experience depicted touches of national reality such as Ghazi Al-Gosaibi and Abdul Rahman Rafi, played the role of a bridge between the past romantic experience and the new wave of poets known as Neo-Realists or Modernists.

4- The Neo- Realist and Modernist Poetry

This new movement in poetry, whose signs emanated from the sixties, can be considered an exit from the dark tunnel or the dim horizon through which all poetic movements in Bahrain passed. This is, of course, after the crushing of the nationalist movement in the fifties and consequently, the exile of its main political leaders, the banning of journals and application of emergency law in the country for ten years. [**22**] Such a banal situation left negative effects on the development of poetry in Bahrain and failed to accord with the novelties of the new poetic movements in the Arab world. However, this stage of confinement and unproductiveness, through which the new poetic movement in Bahrain passed, led eventually to revisions. Furthermore, it promoted action on the basis of various past movements and the contemplation of their poetic elements and patterns, some of which have already been mentioned. This obviously made the Neo-Realist Movement embody a live storehouse of poetic experience in Bahrain. It also equipped poets with opportunities to mediate on the reality of this modern poetic experience in the Arab world and be acquainted with specimens of world poetry and human culture.

After the lifting of the curfew and emergency law in the country in the aftermath of the mid- sixties national political uprising [**23**], the journals recommenced their publication. A new wave of young poets, most of whom descended from the middle and lower social classes, began to reflect on the issues concerning the reality of people and their suffering in their poetry which was imbued with a vein of romantic melancholy and also with a note of extreme optimism. This was obviously an exhibition of their knowledge of the achievements of the New Arabic Poetry whose dawn began to break in a number of Arab countries through some well-known poets, such as Al-Sayaab, Al-Bayati, Nazek, Hawi, Darwish and Abdul Saboor and Hejazi. [**24**]

The prelude to this realization and awareness in poetry became conspicuous, according to the critic Ahmad Al-Mani, when Ali Abdulla Khalifa, [**25**], exposed the tragedy of the sea-divers to the contemporary reader by rendering all its aspects into a poetic subject in his first volume *Moans of the Dhow Masts.*

This was followed by Qasim Haddad's volume of poems *Portents* [**26**] which set out the theme of sad reality through symbolic expressions. Haddad's first volume was characterized by a note of transparency, simplicity and hyper-optimism. The themes were based on human models as well as the sea-divers' experiences. He created an informative framework containing the grim revelation of the local surroundings in a new poetic language based on revolutionary imagery, symbols and themes. Qasim Haddad therefore is, in the critical evaluation of Al-Manai, 'another shining star to broaden this new poetic path and also to emphasize the fact that literature is a means of communication and constant discovery.'

The writer of this introduction, [**27**] according to Al Manai, is a third unique voice in the new-fledged poetry movement with romantic leanings and lyrical tincture. Evaluating the first volume, *Where Does Grief Come From*, Al-Manai concludes that the poems in this collection demonstrate the poet's restraint with the use of language and sound. The poems also illustrate the poet's ability to convey his true experience to his readers through subtle and suggestive statements, and simple-structured phrases.

After these three poets, another group of younger poets entered the arena; their poetry had a touch of variety with an underlining note of the quest for renovation.

The most distinguished of these poets were Yaqoob Al-Muharraqi, Abdul Hamid Al-Qaed, Ali Al-Sharqawi, [**28**] Hamdah Khamis, [**29**] Yousif Hasan, Iman Assiri, and Ibrahim Bu-Hindi. They were followed by another wave of prospective poets whose experience was soon crystallized into various poetic channels. Among them were, Saeed Al-Oweinati [**30**] Ahmad Madan, Ahmad Al-Ajami, Fawzia Al-Sindi, Fathiya Ajlan, Salman Al-Hayki, Fatima Taitoon.

The poetic experience of both Hamdah Khamis and Ali Al-Sharqawi seems to have excelled qualitatively and quantitatively compared to other members of the group. Both have continued to publish numerous volumes of poetry in the past twenty years.

Finally, the familiarity of this new wave of poets with the career and poetry of the well-known Arab poet, Adonis, [**31**] and his influence on them, as was the case with Qasim Haddad before, has moved the new poetic language, in the name of Modernism, in another new direction. Such a move does not seem to accord with the development of the poetic movement in Bahrain with its past features and known characteristics, which enriched the stream of Modern Arabic Poetry.

This is due to the fact that most of these new poetic experiences relied on the association of free imagery which eventually became a governing rule in their experiences. Consequently, such a practice led to the absence of most artistic and literary principles such as form, unity content, rhythm and objectivity. This can be applied to the poetry of the younger generation and in particular to Fawzia Al-Sindi, Ahmad Madan, Ahmad Al-Ajami and Fatima Taitoon. They fell victims to obscure ambiguity, linguistic complexities, surrealistic images, and symbolic expressions. This phenomenon obviously prohibited poetry readers from interacting continuously with such experiences, despite the fact that their poetry carries a dazzling and surprising touch in the use of language and the fluidity of imagery. Nonetheless, such symbolic use of language is not unusual in modern poetry in Bahrain but had deep roots in the poetry of the Classical poets, as noted in the poetry of Al-Zayed.

However, its maturity grew in the poetry of the poets of the sixties and in particular the poetry of Qasim Haddad. He was the one who took one step further than other members of his generation, some of whom preferred silence and some others continued circling round the old traditional and ostentatious use of symbols. This obviously constituted a break in the development of modern poetry whose threads were strongly connected together. It also brought about a halt to the variety of symbolic poetic voices. Hence, the poetry of Qasim Haddad and the symbolic framework became the attraction for the new wave of poets.

A glance at Qasim Haddad's poetry, however, will reveal that his symbols, obscure imagery and vague phrases reflect, in reality, his personality, his heroic struggle and his nationalist and political role even in the Arab world. Added to that, his developed poetic capability in various phases of his artistic career is also noteworthy. It is therefore, the loss of such key factors, or their absence, that may have caused a blockage in the new poetry movement in Bahrain in the last ten years. Obviously, this is due to the fact that there is no clear cause that the new poet can lean on or can write about. Of course this was the case for all the poets in Bahrain starting from Al-Zayani's nationalist movement at the beginning of the twentieth century. Under such circumstances, the new poet is doomed to fall into the same trap as the Romantic poets in Bahrain by avoiding or overstepping the reality of the homeland. Inevitably, such recoil will negatively affect the development of modern poetry in Bahrain today.

Furthermore, lack of poetic experience and inability to apply and practice the main principles of poetic texts, has led the new wave of poets to write prose poetry. The poet, Adonis, was bitterly disappointed with the condition of the prose poem in Arabic Poetry. [**32**] He referred to it in his articles entitled *The Recoil* and *A Text Without Author* where he reviewed this aggravating poetic phenomenon which had spread in the Arab World.

Notes:

* This is an abridged translation of a longer essay entitled 'Contemporary Arabic Poetry in Bahrain'. It was published in Al-Babtein Encyclopaedia, Vol. 6, n.d.

**All footnotes in this anthology are provided by the translator.

1. Quoted by Al-Manai, Ahmad. *An Introduction to the New Literary Movement in Bahrain.*
Originally the Eastern Province was part of the region of Bahrain. Its most historical towns are El-Ehsa and Qatif whose history can be traced back to the Pre-Islamic era. In 1506, the Portuguese invaded the Hurmuz Strait and eventually the Eastern Province. However, they were defeated by the Ottomans in 1550. Weakened by the First World War, the Ottoman Turks withdrew from the Province to let King Abdul Aziz Bin Saud enter it victoriously in 1915.

2. Apart from the commercial significance of these markets, they also had another aspect: the reconciliation of the dialects. The most highly refined dialect was obviously selected and adopted during these literary recitations. It was a proper platform for selecting the lingua franca: the proper dialect to be adopted by poets.

3. The Umayyad dynasty (661 AD–750 AD), attributed to Muaweiah Beni Umayya, the governor of Syria, who appointed himself Caliph after the assassination of the Fourth Caliph, Ali Bin Abi Taleb. The Umayyads were Arab nationalists who severely undermined the importance and the role of other non-Arab Muslims. They revived or consolidated the tradition of court poetry based on the themes of satire, panegyric and love – which were often accompanied by music and dancing. Three well-established poets of this period were: Al-Farazdac, Al-Akhtal and Jarir. The Abbasids (750 AD -1258) claimed to be descended from the Prophet's uncle, Abbas Ibn Abd Al-Muttalib. They defeated the Umayyids in the battle of Zab (750) with the support of the Persians and the Shiites. They moved their capital from Damascus to Baghdad as a sign of cultural and literary assimilation with the Persians. The Abbasid

era is characterized by the works of great Moslem scholars such as Ibn Muqaffa, Al-Khwarizmi, Al- Razi, and Farabi. In the field of poetry, it is sufficient to only mention Bashaar Ibn Burd, Abu Nuwas, Abu Tammam, Al-Buhturi and Abul-Atahiya.

4. This phrase literally means 'outsiders or those who go out' and it refers to a group of Muslims who revolted against the leadership of the Fourth Caliph and the First Shia Imam, Ali Bin Abi Talib, the Prophet's cousin and son-in–law. He was eventually assassinated while performing early morning prayers by Abdul Rahman Bin Muljem, a member of the same clique.

5. Also spelt "Carmathians", "Qarmathians", "Karmathians" and, derived probably from *karmitha* or *karmutha* which meant 'villager' in Southern Iraqi dialect. Other linguists, however, believe that it is derived from *qarmat* meaning 'short-legged person', referring to its leader in Iraq, Hamdan al-Qarmat. In 287, the Qaramathians under the leadership of Abu Sa'id Al-Hasan Bin Bahram al-Jannabi , occupied Bahrain. Later on, he moved from Hajar in Bahrain to El-Ehssa. The Qarmatians were mistakenly attributed to the Ismaelite sect. In fact, they constituted a separate movement with a separate leader. In 317, the Qarmatians led by Abu Tahir, the youngest son, invaded Hijaz, massacred the pilgrims, "choked up the sacred spring of Zamzam, the door of the Kaba was broken open, the veil covering the Kaba was torn down, and the sacred Black Stone was removed from the Kaba and taken to their headquarters at Hajar."

6. It literally means 'negro' or 'black' and it is applied to a group of disgruntled negros in the city of Al-Basrah led by a Shia, Ali Bin Mohammad, who promised to bring social justice and freedom to them. In the beginning, the Zinj were able to defeat the Abbasside Caliphate Al-Mowafaq. In 881, the Caliphate, with the reinforcements from outside, crushed the Zinj and brought the head of the leader Ali Bin Mohammad to Baghdad.

7. A poet of distinct sensibilities, Ali Ibn Al-Muqarab Al-Ayuni was born in El-Ehssa, a principality of the Bahrain region in 1232. He was a descendant of Abdullah Bin Ali Al-Ayuni who defeated the Qaramatha in 1074. Ibn Al-Muqarrab was conscious of the chaotic, or rather tribal nature, of the Uynid dynasty where cousins and brothers fought each other to seize the throne. Though he eulogized most of the Uynid despotic princes, his life was threatened. As a result, he was constantly moving from one region to another, from his homeland El-Ehssa to Iraq and back to Qatif.

8. The Uynid Dynasty came to power in 1074 after defeating Al-Qaramta in El-Ehssa with the support of the Seljuk in Baghdad. They descended from the Abd-Qais tribe which inhabited the Eastern Province of the Arabian Peninsula. The famous

pre-Islamic poet Tarafa Ibn Abd came from the same region. Some historians also speculate that the Arab Shia of Bahrain and the Eastern Province of Saudi Arabia may have descended from the Uynid family and therefore from the same tribe. Abd-Qais tribe were originally Christian but later were converted to Islam and some of its members became staunch followers of Ali Ibn Abi Taleb, the fourth Caliph and the first Shia Imam.

9. The original geographic map of the region of Bahrain comprised Al-Basra, Kuwait, Al-Ehssa, Qatif, Qatar and the Awal islands (present Bahrain).

10. Anti- British protests and demonstrations in the early twenties (1919) by the pearl traders and the Shia majority in Bahrain led to the National Movement of 1923. The British quelled the uprising and expelled the leaders, Sheikh Abdul Wahab Al-Zayani and others to India.

11. The origin of 'Nabat' or 'Nabatean' is controversial. Some scholars associate it with *Al-Anbaat*, a heterogeneous tribe inhabited the lands between Iraq, Jordan and Syria and who spoke *Nabati*, meaning 'a foreign' language. Others are of opinion that it is one of the indigenous dialects of the 'Bedouins' in the Gulf and the Arabian Peninsula. It was called' Nabati' because it sounded different from classical standard Arabic. Whatever the origin, Nabatean poetry does not adhere to the rules of grammar or other linguistic principles. However, it has solid and well-established meters, the best known of which is the Al-Hilali meter, probably referring to the Beni Hilal tribe who first recited Nabatean Poetry.

12. The phrase is often applied to the poetry written in different phases of Arabic literature. Most notably it refers to the pre-Islamic poems which were known as the *muallaqat*, 'the suspended ones', due to their significance and eventually being hung on the wall of the *kaba*. A classical Arabic poem or *qasidah* is usually based on sophisticated rhyme and rhythm, elaborate structure, and a great variety of meters. They include, self-praise, panegyric, satire, elegy, descriptive and courtship or amatory verse. Imagery was derived from the desert surroundings. Poems often begin with a prelude, usually elegiac, describing personal feelings. In the middle, the poet describes his journey and its hardship and the last section is a glorifying note on the bravery or courage of his tribe or the leader.

13. The method of learning the Holy Quran, though pedestrian, it had some interesting qualities which are akin to modern schooling. All learners would start with the initial part of the Holy Quran but only the most arduous and talented ones would be able to complete the whole Book in a short period of time.

14. The world's finest natural pearls came from the Gulf region, the hub of the Sumerian civilization. Bahrain (the Awal islands) became the world's market place for the pearl industry in the early twentieth century. The pearl industry was based, to some extent, on a pyramid system; at the top were the money suppliers who mostly were Asians, then pearl merchants, dhow owners and at the bottom came the sea- divers. Some of the sea-divers were young slaves who were brought from Africa or Baluchistan in Pakistan. However, with the discovery of oil in 1932, the region was turned into a sea channel for the passage of gigantic oil tankers and pollution. The crunch came with the arrival of Japanese cultured pearls which dramatically reduced the price of natural pearls and made thousands of sea-divers redundant. For detailed and recorded reports on sea-diving in the Gulf, see: J.G Lorimer, *The Pearl and Mother of Pearl Fisheries of the Persian Gulf*, Gazetteer of the Persian Gulf, Vol. 1, Historical, Part 2, P.P. 2228 – 2229; Richard Bowen, *Pearl Fisheries of the Persian Gulf*, The Middle East Journal, Spring 1951, Vol. 5 No. 2. P.161; Durand, E.L. *Notes of the Pearl Fisheries of the Persian Gulf*, 8th July 1878, the Persian Gulf Administration Reports, Vol.1, P.35; C.D Belgrave, *The Pearl Industry of Bahrain*, 10 Dec. 1928, Records of the Persian Gulf Pearl Fisheries, Vol. 2. P.533 & Pelly L., *Political Resident*, Circular No.9, 16 Sept. 1868, Records of the Persian Gulf Pearl Fisheries, Vol.1, P.13.

15. The British colonial occupation of Bahrain goes back to 1820. As Portuguese power gradually weakened, the British consolidated their control of the island and other islands in the Gulf. It formally became a British Protectorate in 1861 and was granted independence on 15th August 1971.

16. Initially, 'spots' of Romanticism in Modern Arabic Poetry may be traced in the poetry of the Lebanese poet, Khalil Mutran (1872-1949) whose disillusionment with the Neo-Classical poets led to his call for innovations in Arabic poetry. However, it was his two Egyptian disciples, Ahmad Zaki Abu Shadi (1892-1955) and Ibrahim Naji (1899-1953) who pioneered the Romantic Movement in the Arab World. Physicians by profession, the two poets laid a solid foundation of Romantic theories in Arabic Poetry, basically inspired by their knowledge and experience of Western literature, and, in particular, English Romantic poetry.

17. One of the most ill-fated Arab poets of the twentieth century. Al-Askar was born in Kuwait in 1917, into a religious family. He completed his schooling at Al-Mubarakia school, which was the first formal school in Kuwait. Al-Askar began writing poetry at an early age; he was a keen and avid reader of philosophical books. Eventually, his religious inclinations began to fade away. Another critical event in his life was his addiction to alcohol which he celebrated and considered his poetic inspiration. The drifting away of his ideological beliefs, on the one hand, and his

excessive consumption of alcohol, on the other hand, isolated Al-Askar from his family and society. He was accused of being an infidel and apostate. Consequently, he lost his sight and fell ill. On 15 August 1951, Al-Askar died; at his funeral there were only five people, including the grave digger and the preacher. The greatest loss was the burning of his writings by his family. Al-Askar's poetry is characterized by a sense of melancholy and emotional outbursts. His rebellious spirit and his disbelief in social norms, the desertion of his friends and family, and eventually his tragic and miserable death, all of these make Al-Askar a true child of Romanticism.

18. His translation of Omar Khayyam's *Quartets* is considered a classic. Two other Arab scholars, among many, who excelled in their translation of Khayyam's *Quartets,* were the Iraqi Ahmad Safi Al-Najafi and the Egyptian Ahmad Rami..

19. Gazi Al-Gosaibi was born in Saudi Arabia and is presently a Saudi citizen. He held various academic, diplomatic and ministerial positions in Saudi Arabia. His inclusion among Bahraini poets by Dr. Alawi Al-Hashmi as in this Introduction and his Anthology of *Contemporary Poets of Bahraini* may be irrelevant and superfluous. Apparently, Dr. Al-Hashmi relied more or less on Ghazi Al-Gosaibi's early education which took place in Bahrain and his early poetic career which is considered a landmark in the rise of the Neo-Romanticism movement in Bahrain. Nevertheless, territorial identity or demarcation is a hot issue in literary affairs nowadays and still there are unsolved cases of these 'suspended' poets or writers of whom T.S. Eliot's is an obvious example.

20. Abdul Rahman Rafi is nowadays better known as a serious colloquial poet. His poems in the Bahraini Gulf dialect, are often fused with a sense of bitter humour, has won him striking fame in the region.

21. Ali Mahmoud Taha (1902-1949) and Omar Abu Reesha (1910-1990) are two lyric poets who introduced non-traditional themes and images into twentieth century Arabic poetry. Taha's poetry is characterized by a sense of longing for the unknown as in his *The Lost Mariner* (1934) and *The Nights of the Lost Mariner* (1940) often displayed in a hedonistic vein. Abu Reesha, on the other hand, found the themes of politics and women of great interest in his poetry.

22. The impact of the Egyptian Revolution of 1952, and in particular its charismatic leader Jamal Abdel Nasser, on the Arab populace was outstanding. The nationalist movement which began in the fifties in Bahrain was a direct response to Nasser's call for Arab unity and his fight against colonialism. On 13 October, 1954 the Shia as well as Sunni leaders met in Al-Khamis Mosque to draft a united agenda against British colonial rule. The whole island was boiling with Nasser's' slogans. The movement,

however, was crushed by the British and its leaders, Abdul Rahman Al-Baker, Abdul Aziz Al-Shamlan and Abdul Ali Al-Alaywat were expelled to the island of St. Helena on 23 December 1956. Furthermore, the British landed troops, announced emergency law and banned journals. Apparently, what exasperated the British most was the incident that happened to Selwyn Lloyd, the British Foreign Secretary in Bahrain on his way to Cairo: his car was stoned by the angry people shouting against Sir Charles Belgrave who later was released from his duties as Advisor to the Ruler.

23. If the Nasserites and the Arab nationalists monitored the uprising of the fifties against the British, it was the Bahrain Patriotic Liberation Front (renamed recently the Democratic & Progressive Tribune) and other Marxist Fronts which planned the strikes and the demonstrations of the workers and the students in the sixties. Furthermore, if the first two groups excluded Bahraini members of Persian origin from their activities, the Bahrain Patriotic Liberation Front was a replica or a continuation of the Iranian Tuda (Communist) Party whose founders were Bahrainis of Persian descent. In March 1965, the whole of Bahrain was paralyzed by student demonstrations and strikes by BAPCO (Bahrain Petroleum Company) workers. That was a response to the company's decision to sack more than 400 Bahraini workers. More than 10 Bahrainis were killed by the British, tens of students and workers were imprisoned or exiled.

24. Badr Shaker Al-Sayyab (1926-1964); Nazek Al-Malaeka (1923- 2007); Abdul Wahab Al-Bayati (1926-1999); Khalil Hawi (1919-1982); Mahmud Darwish (1942-2008); Salah Abdul Saboor (1931-1981); Ahmad Abdul Mu'ti Hejazi (1935-).

25. Ali Abdulla Khalifa is one of the most socially committed Bahraini poets of this century; a poet of powerful sensitivity and astounding ability to delineate undiluted and vivid pictures of past and present Bahraini society in his poetry. However, he has gone through an unprecedented shift of themes and vocabulary in his recent collection which is, indeed a reflection of the poet's transitional outlook.

26. Qasim Haddad is a poet of great artistic innovations; he is certainly, the most innovative poet in the Gulf region. The influence of twentieth century Arab poets, such as Al-Sayyab and Adonis is traceable in his poetry. In his early poetry, social and political messages are skilfully woven within mythical allusions. His reference to the Greek hero, Sisyphus, who defied Zeus, is an illustration of the poet's profound knowledge of world literature. His experiments with haiku poetic forms and concrete poetry in recent years, is an indication of the poet's endeavours to align himself with current developments in contemporary literature.

27. Alawi Al-Hashmi is the Greek Adonis of contemporary Bahraini poetry: he proclaimed poetic death at an early stage of his poetic career and after publishing only two collections of poems, *Where does Grief come from* in 1972 and *Sparrows and the Shade of Tree* in 1978. His poetry is characterized by a sense of nostalgia and a strong craving and longing for the past. Nevertheless, and despite his poetic hibernation, Alawi Al-Hashmi has produced some outstanding critical studies on Bahraini Poetry; the most noticeable is the *Anthology of Contemporary Poets of Bahrain* which was published in 1988.

28 A prolific writer; a highly productive poet of amazing caliber. Al-Sharqawi has published more than twenty volumes of poetry, several plays and numerous articles in local journals. In his recent poetry, his grievance at the haunting of the past is subdued and, instead, there is the spirit of compromise and reconciliation.

29. Hamdah Khamis embodies in her poetry a genuine and sincere 'Penelope image' of Bahraini women: the theme of waiting exudes through her lines with natural exuberance. It echoes the Henderson era where thousands of Bahraini writers were arrested, leaving their mothers, wives and daughters waiting for their release.

30. Saeed Al-Oweinati was mercilessly tortured to death by Ian Henderson, Head of the Intelligence Service and his squad in Bahrain, on 12 December 1976.

31. Ali Ahmad Saeed (1930-) was born in Syria and was an active member of the Syrian Nationalist Party. He was imprisoned for his political activities and later fled to Lebanon. He adopted the pen name Adonis (the handsome Greek youth who was slain by a wild boar in Greek Mythology) in his early poetic career. Undoubtedly, he is the pioneer of New Poetry in the Arab world. His provocative pronouncements against the Arab authorities, his constant call for radical change and innovation in Modern Arabic Poetry made Adonis the muse and poet-idol of young Arab poets all over the Arab world. His poetry, like his personality, has traversed the path of Shellean social and political dissent, in particular in his early career as in *The Earth Has Said* to the land of total visionary, surrealist and mystic grounds as in *Songs of Mihyar the Damascene* (1961) *The of Metamorphosis* and *Migration in the Regions of Day and Night* (1965) and *Time Between Ashes and Roses* (1970).

32. Prose poetry is a new phenomenon in Modern Arabic poetry. The first prose poem was published in Al-Shir (Poetry) magazine by the Lebanese poet Ansi Al-Haj in 1958 under the influence of the French poet Saint- Jean Perse. But it was the Syrian/Lebanese poet Adonis who designated the term 'prose' and defined it as 'a new expression, and 'a new writing' which becomes 'a rhythmical metrical prose or a blend of metrical prose and other elements'. However, a prose poem is definitely

inconsistent with the classical definition of poem or *qasidah* or even free verse because of the lack of line or stanza division within its structure. Adonis, nevertheless, warned modern Arab poets of misinterpreting and misapplying of prose poetry by thinking that it is 'a climax of modernism' and hence disregarding rhythm and meter in a revolt against traditional poetry.

Works Cited

(All references in this Introduction are translated from the original Arabic titles).

Al-Ansari, Jaber. "Studies in Modern Bahraini Literature." *Hunna Al-Bahrain Journal* Dec. 1966:168.

..., *Glimpses of the Gulf*. Bahrain, 1970.

Al-Bahrani, Husain Bin Sheikh Ali. *The Garden of Eulogy and Lament*. India, 1920

Adonis, "The Recoil." *Al-Hayat Journal* 24 Mar. 1994: n. p..

...,"A Text Without Author." *Al-Hayat Journal* 7 Apr. 1994: n. p.

Al-Hashmi, Alawi. *What Has the Palm-tree Said to the Sea: A Critical Study of Contemporary Poetry in Bahrain*. Dar El-Huriya: Iraq, 1981.

Al-Jeshi, Hasan Jawad. Al-Arrayedh: "The Pioneer of Romanticism in the Gulf." *Sada El-Esbu* 1971.

Al-Khalifa, Mai . *The Lord of Writers in Bahrain: Ibrahim Bin Mohammad Al-Khalifa (1850- 1923).* Bahrain,1993.

Al-Khater, Mubarak. *The Genius of Bahrain: Abdulla Al-Zayed.* Bahrain,1972

..., The Islamic Forum. Bahrain, 1981

Al-Manai, Ahmad. *An Introduction to the New Literary Movement in Bahrain*. Bahrain, 1973.

Al-Reihani, A. *Kings of Arabia* Beirut, 1990.

Al-Tai, Abdullah. *Contemporary Literature in the Arabian Gulf* Cairo: Institute of Arabic Studies, 1974.

IBRAHIM AL-ARRAYEDH

A Debate with Existentialism [1]

You were absorbed in self-conceit
To the height of supremacy;
Towards me you were eventually led, indeed.
I saluted your beauty with my blessings wholeheartedly.

1

How many times I wandered in the bushes,
Missed by not returning the whole night.
But they surprised me with a lover's blushes
Unveiling to his beloved her charming sight.

2

Is this glamour only apparent on earth
Revives itself as years pass by me?
Whilst above, the planets in adornments bathe,
Thus I ask: who possess such glee?

3

Is not the answer self-evident like a glowing face
Anxious for a beloved's unity?
Whose smile is sweetened by tears' grace,
For truth is above imagination's superiority.

4

Risen from the clay to a naked thorn's span
Until a shy rose transpires;
Must be a sign for a distant plan
Evolution is the hope to which every man aspires.

5

For life as darkness is dreary
Without flare,
If ever I live for your love calmly,
Like an ember on a log I dare to pray.

6

I kissed your eyes whilst about to dream,
Never took long time
To be enthralled with an eternal beam
Where sunset and sunrise together climb.

7

Be patient, for love is a chance
To expose her reality:
That is the truth, not a symbol at which to glance;
In art, love is the spring of beauty.

My Angel

Ask the light whether the moon,
A story of her mother and her told.
Cheerfully smiling to him [**2**]
The mother beheld
And towards me she hastened to convey her delight.
In a wonder she exclaimed
Of her daughter's laughter in disguise!
Two pearls were displayed on her mouth
And one on her cheeks shined.
I approached the cradle with a glance;
It was Hind [**3**] whose mother awaited her in advance.
Not moved by heavenly words
But like a smiling bud joyfully lied.
Wrapped in merriment like a gazelle
As light as a bird flies.
Heedless of objects around,
As if in a pit her hands dig to find.
Or on her foot a hand is seen
Touching it lightly;
Excitingly, she removes the mark
And laughs like a lovely rose enveloped
In a secret smile.
Not more than a whisper,
Her laughter like a light touch of string runs
And in her cry she appears like roses,
Misted in pearls by rain clouds,

In her eyes heaven resides;
Twinkle and shine all the stars.
What an ecstasy our love is filled with
To view beauty under the moonlight.
Like Hind's image as she glances at us
With a floating smile on her mouth,
In vain we try to make it hide.
How many times her mother
Dispersed kisses,
In the shade I leant to pick some up.
My angel! You are preserved in my love
And between you two, I am the luckiest!

A Skylark

Warbling in the horizon indeed,
It appears so small like a star;
As fast as the speed of the wind,
In the open air it flies afar.
Beating on the ears its light flutter
To travel with the wind in azure
Sky more than a mile.
But soon it is overcome with melancholy;
The sound dwindles away little by little.
Ah, my skylark!
What a great melody you excel at in the air?
Bringing to silence all other melodies nearby?

Only to ease yourself down
When your enthralled spirit is thrown
Into ecstasy high.
And as the sound of the strings diminishes [**4**]
Its echo in the hearts lasts forever;
Unaware of its creator, Nature is in slumber,
Only to be awakened by you as His messenger.
A wonder you've accomplished
A shielded shade your are, indeed,
For the orchard to cherish hereafter.
You've taught us a secret of Beauty,
Without which never will we the beauty of life
Realize:
That no roses in nature blossom a while,
But only on a tear of your joyful melody;
For you turn their sorrow into a smile
With your songs of everlasting eternity. [**5**]

1. The transcendent tone that prevails in this poem is indeed reminiscent of Rabindranath Tagore's *Gitanjali* which was most probably read by Al-Arrayedh.

2. 'him' refers to the moon

3. Hind is the name of the poet's second daughter

4. Ibrahim Al-Arrayed's use of figures of speech, in particular metaphor and simile as in this poem, is truly remarkable. Indeed, if we agree with I. A. Richard's theory, that in a metaphor interest lies in the "disparity" rather than the "analogy", then the qualities that Ibrahim Al-Arrayedh has attributed to Hind, are so sublime that they are not shared by other vehicles (metaphoric words) in the poem.

5. The Wordsworthian 'inward eye' can be easily traced in this poem. It is an outcry of both wild imagination and unrestrained emotion. One of the reasons for Al-Arrayedh's familiarity with English Romantic tenets and temperament was his early education in India where the school curriculum, until recently, was based on the study of English 'canonical' texts and writers such as Shakespeare, Milton, Wordsworth and Hardy.

AHMAD MOHAMMED AL-KHALIFA

The Sea-diver's Ode [1]

I am the diver in the sea,
Patience and diligence my allies be.

With the furious wind I drive
In attacks and retreats I always survive.

My old age taught me
With courage and patience to have glee.

With an ambitious heart I am sealed
To free work I yield.

I am the son of far distant waves:
Who in darkness and in dawn craves.

With the wind I strove indeed,
And in early age my songs did lead.

I saw whales in deep seas swimming
But I had no fear or sighs of their coming.

Hasan Marhamah

My dhow at night sails
Amongst waves and rocks it trails.

Unaware of the wind's fierce fleets
My delightful heart with hopes beats.

As though with Suleiman my companion hails
Over his magic rag avails.

In deep seas I dive
For rare pearls I strive.

And sing joyful songs
At night and sunrise all along.

And murmur sadly:
How it was a long time,
Since friends sailed happily.

1. This is a poem of celebration and jubilance compared to Ali Abdulla Khalifa's poem *Moans of the Dhow Masts*. Both focus on the subject of sea-diving but with two distinct perspectives; the first depicts the joy and pride of the sea-diver and the second exhibits the sense of separation, alienation and eventually death of the sea-diver.

ABDUL RAHMAN RAFI

She Grew on Sands

My beloved,
The sun in her land
Is a river of illumination;
It is devoid of the blessings of the sky
And the laughter of the spring and the fruit.
But, the gust of the wind in it
Creates beauty,
For my beloved grew on sands.

In the crowds, I was put down by fate,
Carrying within my ribs
A heart of tears.
And it was on the road,
My beloved,
That you appeared;
On the strange and forlorn road of my life
Like a green oasis on the verge of bareness.
Wearied… I began to sing of salvation in the vastness
Of your paradise.
But a voice,
From behind the dense-echoed horizon,
As the whisper of annihilation in the ruined graves,

Hasan Marhamah

Surrounded me
With horrible gales
Asking me to stop,
For I was not born for the spring.
Woe to those who live in the spring
And do not feel the joy of life in the spring.

So you, my beloved,
Whilst in dream of happiness,
Remember that I am in grief,
In a struggle with yearnings,
Without companion and in the depth of agony.
I walk towards
The drowned shore,
There, where suffering is born,
I rest my face on my hand,
And let my palm
Draw in the spring of tears.

AHMAD AL-SHAMLAN *

An Invitation to a Forbidden Party

My apology to you my good friends:
My party is poor
For I spent what I earned on my future journeys.
Exhausted, I arrived carrying my drowned guitar
With a melody you have heard before,
When it was captive
And you were the lyrics in the depressing jails,
While the thug gurgled his anger;
His crushed nails tortured my guitar and flirted with his whips:
A poem smiled.
My apology, the music may not be continued in a small party.

****

I fetched you tonight palm wine,
Do you like dates?
I posses nothing but this vintage liquor;
I stole it,
It is condensed but genuine;
Those who sold its tree never became intoxicated,
But I was intoxicated by an infant.
What shall I say?
In my eye there was an impossible question,
Wandering through long nights but never fulfilled…

A candle in a beautiful one-time party.
But they have changed my home address;
My home is a melody tonight,
A distraction in a small dream
And I fear the street guards.

The street guards have plotted against me,
They have changed my home address.
My friends
Come in,
I have for you
Liquor
Reproach
And joy.

A Rainbow Hymn

Extend a bridge from the sea to grief so to reach me,
And some whisper to silence to enrich me;
Exhausted, my hands are stretched towards you
So come closer, don't reject me.
Alas! The silence of storm has been expanded and prolonged,
It drew me on the wave's wall a pictorial souvenir,
Promised me to move the holes of whispers closer and closer from one wall to another.
And I, calling the walls to pour a letter,
And separate the walls from the glimpse of light,
So I can embrace it for a moment,
And light my candles and walk in a barren darkness
And sing in ecstasy.

Ah, my exiled light! You have come back to me.
So welcome to the adventurer;
The manacles never delayed you
From the date of my happiness;
The police stations could not delay you.
Ah, my bird, take caution:
Pierce the walls at night
And spread silence in the evening,
You alone are haunted by joy
And surrounded by fire.
You alone are engraved on the walls and the cables,
From which directions does joy come to you?
The morning of my adventurous bird has prevailed,
It is morning and not evening that embraces us.
I became addicted to the remaining walls
And I patted gently on the back of my silence
And spoke whenever speech arose;
My senility has departed with darkness:
We both became intimate with restrictions or chasing
And sobbing silence.
We both debated the walls and the poem
And poured colours on the butterflies
And changed the seasons;
Time soon will be nearer
And clearer.
My appointment has arrived for the journey of joy
For the sake of her eyes.

Hasan Marhamah

It is my face and the address of my waiting,
So extend to me a thread with the breath of joy:
My appointment tonight is to embrace the rainbow.

*One of the most highly revered and celebrated nationalists in the history of modern Bahrain. An outspoken Communist, Ahmad Al-Shamlan began his political activities at an early age. He was an influential figure in the March 1965 uprising. Consequently, he was imprisoned, tortured and sent into exile. Upon his return, Al-Shamlan was kept under constant house surveillance until he suffered a stroke in 1996. He was not allowed to seek treatment and eventually suffered speech retardation. In his poems the theme of victory is often depicted in the image of light which is a salient feature of his poetry.

YOUSIF HASAN

The Sleeping Village

My comrades,
I feel that I waste away,
And a mysterious thing
Within me
Leads me towards the sunset: [**1**]
Burns the palm trees in my garden,
Gnaws away the tree,
Plucks my eye's light
To extinguish the moon.

My comrades,
I feel something mysterious within me
Akin, perhaps, to the Moguls [**2**]
Whose horses pound my veins,
Uproot my depth
And the fields' crops.
It watches over us open-mouthed,
Asks about what the gazes whisper,
Pierces through darkness
And crucifies the sleeping people. [**3**]

Hasan Marhamah

I feel my comrades,
A weighty tread:
Like that of hypocrisy,
Murdering in our land
The innocent doves,
And in our youths,
Manhood's buds;
Extinguishing the candles,
Causing the gardens to whither
From dampness and the loss of roses.

I feel my comrades,
The sellers' incense in our land
Is like vomit in our mouths,
Tuberculosis in our chests
And a legion of locusts
Nibbling what mankind plant.

I feel my comrades,
I waste away in a village which is
Ignorant of what yearnings and sunrise are,
In a slumberous village,
Ignorant of what love and dreams are,
But prays to God and calls for peace,
Protection and peace.

I feel my comrades
I waste away,
Like my fallen love in the middle of the road,
Swept by the wind,

And like a song
Trembles on the eyelashes of a dying girl
In my village,
Which was and is,
Women are doomed to death
And men to prison …

1. 'Sunset' here connotes 'death'.

2. The Moguls' invasion of the Islamic lands was seen as barbaric and devastating. The attack and looting of Baghdad by the Mogul king Hulagu in 1258 C.E.) is a good example of their atrocity. In Modern Arabic Poetry the term is often associated with despotic and tyrannous rulers.

3. The village is the microcosm of the homeland which is threatened and is on the verge of annihilation. .

ALI ABDULLA KHALIFA

Moans of the Dhow Masts

Alas! They have sailed.
Woe to sorrow,
Woe to what permeates my depths
And rages in madness.
Woe to the days fed on suffering
By deserting my frail and crumbled body.
Here, they are sailing... all comrades,
Ebullient at first.
Their oars pierce the sea
Fiercely and harmoniously,
While the masts moan
Together with the sailors' song **[1]**
In a melancholic cadence
That is unbearable.

Loneliness and the grief of the evening,
The roars of the waves and the women's chatter.
And the fall of a pure tear from a child's eye,
Who is in the torment of fever.
There is a question in his eyes
Which penetrates into the depths
And is hoarse and full of expectations.
Ah, father, when is the return?
Perhaps ,there is no return. **[2]**

A dignified giant,
A man thrown on the shore like a dead body,
Wiped out by the sea,
And driven back by the despot's laws
After having lived his prime years crucified
Among his starving children
And a caller demanding his debts. [**3**]

How my inexperienced heart wept of fear
When first as a Tabaab I left for the sea? [**4**]
My mother bid me farewell with tears
And lots of advice.
My father, praying to God, wishing me
Adulthood soon,
And to bear the burden of family by travelling beyond,
In quest of pearls
Which would seduce the wandering Tawaash.[**5**]
Or, by fortune I may come across Dana [**6**]
Whose beauty fascinates every sea-diver,
The sheer sight of the shell's heart will make me pose
Like a worshipper, perhaps for the first and the last time.
And the soft hand would stretch its hired touch [**7**]

Only to retreat,
Causing sorrow to rise in my broken heart
Leaving my ill-fortune the food for my starving children.
In the day time, I live with the crowds,
Watching the sea and filling the tobacco leaf for a daring diver
Who unwillingly probes and is struck
By the depths of the sea
And beheld the hands of the divers…
Bruised of salt and blood-stained of ropes.
And the night falls after an exhausting day
With frustrated stars in the sky
And trembling shadows.
There is silence every where except for the divers' coughs [**8**]
And the moans and the prayers.
My night is spent in frantic visions
With illusions around me and the unbearable apparitions,
Frightening the heart and weakening determination.

*****

As time passed by swiftly,
Experience taught me the art of diving;
I fell in love with the sea.
And grew the intimacy between us.
My insatiable yearnings for the land diminished,
As arose within me a strong love for the sea.
I was about to keep the sight of my children and my heart behind
And live all my life sailing with my companions,
Sharing equally the daily bread,
Bestowed on us by God.

*****

Sailing needs strength
And my body is frail.
The oars reject my palms with contempt
Forever.
Ah sea,
Why should I grieve now?
When the crowds joining the knots of the mast,
Pointed at me,
At the time of departure
Crying "God be with you... our meeting is soon"?
Then I waved.
Tears covered my face as the masts began to moan, [**9**]
To give company to the divers' song
Which was melancholic and intolerable.

****

Ah sea,
Our tales are never-ending,
Wearied by the night
And discarded by the noon.
Diving has exhausted me,
But still is my captor.
Here I have been created
As a left-over ... of a despised refuse. [**10**]

Hasan Marhamah

Traces of Feet on the Water (Fragment)

And we awaited you for a long time…
I and the night
And the city's wall
The windows in every lane;
Silence was made impossible
For there were eyes around me
And eagerness was pulsating in these eyes:
The pulses of expectations.
We waited for you with the star
Which penetrated the dark clouds with the Shamaal wind [**11**]
And we smelled…
The downpour of scent from the bending dawn,
Expecting you to arrive with the sunrise.

The lovers sang amidst smoke and ashes,
But the day passed by and you never appeared
Like a lover carrying love to a captured beloved;
The gossips slashed us,
Cultivated in us mirage-like plants.
We became agitated,
And hid ourselves in narrow cracks,
Waiting for your pulse-burnt mother
To continue her wasted quest in barren lanes,
Disclosing to passers-by her far distant grief
By asking the walls: Has Obeid come back?

Sunk in the bottom of time,
I ran towards the comrades,
Sensing revolution in them
And tiredness:
Wearily, I prolonged my stay
In anger's facial expression:
Perhaps another wound covered your wound
-Who then removed the soil from the wound?
-They took him with the wound? [**12**]
The hired soldier aimed his gun at him, [**13**]
Trod on the lamps' debris,
The roses fell,
Fell on the ground, a star
Coloured the earth,
Wriggled and then relaxed:
We scattered on different sides…
Wish I had been armed that day.

In the Farewell of the Green Lady

When the tide drowns you **[14]**
And the tar obliterates your image,
You will remain a feeble stem in the depth of the brown soil…
A life memory for millions of lofty trees:
The mistresses of the endowed One.

Hasan Marhamah

You have been betrothed to the sea,
The sea that burns in passion,
And kneels for a wounded person,
Washes the feet with love
And departs.
But if it emerged,
You would drink the salt tear:
You were the servant of the house,
A shelter for the exhausted and those who languished,
A mother for the poor.

Whenever wilderness expanded on the earth,
Your root would remain permanent and durable;
For the clouds' drizzle will bring you near
To the lake's greetings,
To the sea and
To Heaven.

What can I say to a child dozing on my lap
When he glances at a shadow of your remains on the edges
Of the fields?
And sings some frantic melodies
Which will soon vanish
Because of the sufferings nursed by the poets?
Ah, my green lady,
What can be done?
The world departs from its green colour
And the earth which had once a ceremony of seedlings,

Killed its warm feelings

And said to the hollow-men:

Bring forth what has remained from cement and tar?

1. *Niham* or the lead singer whose responsibility it was to console the pearl- divers by singing melancholic and motivating songs

2. The pearl- diving season lasted for six months. During these months, divers were required to dive all day without any paid wages; they had one meal, usually rice and fish. The chances of returning home was minimal as the danger of the sea, the sun and human deceases made their survival almost impossible

.

3. The divers were not paid wages but usually would either share the profit or take a loan from the dhow chief, *Nokhadah*. Such economic exploitation led eventually to some reforms in pearl industry in 1924.

4. *Tabaab* is a young boy often employed to be trained in sea diving and to assist the sea- divers. He is only given food but no wages.

5. *Tawaash* is the sea -merchant who sails in his private boat in hope of buying the pearls from the *Nokhadah*, the chief , before they are brought to the land.

6. *Danna* is a pearl of medium size, but of the finest quality.

7. It is the sea -diver who laboriously reaches the depths of the sea to get the pearl but he is never able to own it.

8. In addition to physical diseases such as mouth and ear infections, lung and heart problems, sunburn and arthritis, the sea -divers were also exposed to psychological and mental disorders.

9. The departure of the sea divers is decried as a funeral procession; the journey will take more than three months and there is uncertainty about the divers' safe return home.

10. After ten dives a day for almost four months at a depth of 30-50 feet in the sea, with only dates, rice and fish as their diet, the sea -divers according Belgrave's report

published in 1928, usually did not live long. They looked like distorted corpses with various skin scars and ulcers.

11. A summer north-westerly wind blowing over the Gulf with large sandstorms.

12. The personal memory of the wound, the icon of suffering of the past, gradually becomes a collective memory. Ali Abdulla Khalifa transforms these historical memories into the memories of the poor and the oppressed. The wound therefore emerges as a mirror through which the mourning of the whole community is reflected.

13. A reference to the March 1965 uprising and the death of one of the militants by a foreign mob.

14. The green lady is the old green Delmon: pure, spotless and pristine land with its beautiful farms, natural pools and orchards which no longer exists. The verdant land and the fertile soil have been drastically erased to keep pace with the fast rise in construction buildings; instead, only the memory remains in the form of an absent green lady.

ALAWI AL-HASHMI

The Floods (Fragment)

(...the journey that my grandfather was dreaming of)

Where does grief come from
And you are with me?
Where does it come from?
A choked candle gleams,
Cries amidst the labyrinth of the night.
A shaky shadow climbs its stature
Stretches, expands,
Spreads out in the desert;
Lets the worm crawl under its black gown,
Nests in the pupils of the crucified
Who survive on the dreams of the crown.
Red icons, like blood's colour
With the taste of blood:
Death's shadow stretches out
On the painful chest of the dancing candle
But not taking long,
It tumbles
Contracts like mercury
And evaporates like illusion.

Hasan Marhamah

The crawling worm is in fright [**1**]
Fleeing, searching for a hole
To be protected from fear,
And the crucified in the dreams of the crown,
Surge in multitude
Walk
 in resentment and excitement
(Is there any one among us who is not crucified?
And is not in pain?)
Where does, then, grief come from?
Where does it come from?
And you are with me?

The Exit from the Circle of Unconsciousness

My memory is laden with yesterday's woes: [**2**]
It was an evening…
And the coffee-shop as usual was thronged with stone-gazed people:
People with chronic defects,
And homosexuals,
And some villagers with sun-burnt faces.
The waiter, like the clock's needle,
Walked in the commotion of the crowd.
While the old lovers' place
Was empty in the corner.

(Why does the face of century turn old and the lover's face remains young?)
The eyes of the hounds were searching for their seats;
Some workers scattered here and there
And a bus broke the silence of the street.
The waiter in the noise of the coffee-shop
Walked to and fro,
Like the clock's needle.
Mansour reclined his palms against the back seat
Leant on his left elbow
And surrendered to his dream:
It was autumn…
And the western wind ravaged
The erect tree;
Only some leaves were left behind
Sweeping…
(Was it really autumn?
Was it evening?
Today's grief will not separate me from that of tomorrow,
And no human will distance me from what will happen tomorrow
Nor will it take away the awakened one,
So close to my surrounding,
From my fallen time on the bed of distance)

And on the fringe of the stretched eyelashes, flickers a green string…
Another era emerges
To be planted under the shell
While the tree-like body reconstructs its cells…
The sun shines…the cloud arrives and the earth lurks in the shadows.
(Do trees die?
Was it really autumn?
Was it evening?)

The commotion in the coffee shop, the stony gazes, the homosexuals standing in queue,
The suspended workers, the trees, the new and old lovers,
The villagers.. the bus, the road…
Mansour falls asleep,
He opens his eyes when the waiter asks him:
Do you want to drink anything?

A Song to a Woman Who Resembles the Homeland (Fragment)

-1-

When at a distance I sang to her my yearnings,
And overwhelmed her with my hidden feelings,
Then with sad handkerchief she waived to me
And as the wind she dashed away
She did not hear me then,
As though she had never been aflame
With the sorrows of the city
Ere this day.
This quenching forehead and eyes, [**3**]

Of legendary beauty and grief,
Of hidden glow in the chest,
She rushed like the wind inattentive.
Her poetic memory has been robbed from her,
She walked away inattentive
The passion for songs
Has been robbed from her mouth,
The day they sealed her lips with the law.
She walked away,
Along the pathway,
In attentive.

-2 -

Where is your destination my lady?
Where are you walking to?
The wound is still in flame,
The sorrows expand with time,
And the tender moments
Drip in the heart
Successively.
Here the trees of life and youth pose nude,
No longer do the lovers' palm-trees soothe…
For they have been uprooted by hot sandstorms
So where is your direction, the lady of lovers
Whilst around you the earth's waist is pierced with groans.

1. The image of the worm here is reminiscent of T.S. Eliot's poem 'The Love Songs of J. Alfred Prufrock' where Prufrock recollects:

'The eyes that fix you in a formulated phrase,
And when I am formulated, sprawling on a pin,
Where I am pinned and wriggling on the wall,'

2. This poem, as its title suggests, is a revelation of inner conflicts; a monologue of total despair. Alawi Al-Hashmi probes deep into the mind of his alter ego to unravel the forces that occupy the sub-conscious.

3. She is able to quench her feelings quickly

HAMDAH KHAMIS *

You Have Your Own Time, I Have Mine

Ah, mother,
I awaited you a century,
A century of horror and
Of longing.
I said to myself when you were late:
You will certainly arrive in the next season.
I said: certainly you will.
And I surrendered my dream,
The dream of waiting,
To your forthcoming offspring.

I met a child's smile at the crossroads;
I leant with my wound and the heart's sigh.
I met them;
They were drawing childhood on the prison's wall,
Reading the book to you
From love… or from a chapter of blood.
And when I felt their deep yearnings
I said: this is the beginning of the roads
To the destination of water;
And I realized that
You will certainly arrive,
My mother.

The lashes wheeze on the skins
And your naked and starving children are
On their move towards you,
Towards the road of the oppressed.
And I realized then that
You will certainly arrive,
For the sea's gazes of longing,
Mirror your arrival
And the palm-trees' celebration begins with the newly born. [**1**]
The dawn has given a promise
And the sun has given a promise;
There is a season for the sap to grow,
Which will restore the early life of the Caliph
Will sprout in him the leaves of certainty.
And you, mother,
You will arrive.

We know
That these swords are directed at your path,
These whips,
These prisons
And we, mother,
We will move towards you
Under the swords
The whips
And through the prisons
And you will be there…

Preparing for the departure
So for you, we expand
The bridge of grief.
For you, mother, we expand the bridge of dream;
And you are the dream.
You are a faraway dream
And … a soon- fulfilled dream.
You are the passion we long for,
The passion which is my first road towards you,
We long for it.
Do you wish to cross your children's bridge now
To the bridge of your forthcoming children?
I dreamt at night,
Reading to you the incantation of starvation;
-I was swimming on the banks of fire-
And in the ebb of darkness.
I washed myself with your water,
Moved towards your direction,
Murmured your name,
And I realized that:
For killing there is a time
For terror there is a time
For subjugation there is a time
For starvation there is a time
There is a time to prohibit breathing.
Ah, mother,
Between me and the law
There is the Judgment Day,

Hasan Marhamah

For any law there is a time
For every law there is a night when the frogs croak.
But these do not last long;
You will stay
I will stay,
And all your bright hungry children
Will stay,
For you will become a constitution for all periods.

*This is an early poem by Hamdah Khamis. One of the recurrent images in her poetry and in this poem, in particular, is that of children. She often delineates with clarity and precision the fate of children whose parents are either in exile or in prison.

1. The image of palm-trees is one of the prominent images in contemporary Bahraini poetry. On the one hand, it connotes the advent of the era of victory which is often accompanied by the celebrations of children; on the other hand, it is the symbol of the cross on which the martyrs are nailed

ABDUL HAMID AL-QAED

Grief of a Winter Night

Ah, the woman of shadow,
Of which sorrows shall I talk to you?
For the trembling grief in my heart
Carries the mask of death and the colour of water;
A sad child,
A man…
A chaste woman,
A frenzied love
That the falls flung in the world river.
Only the strange lovers know it
And I am alone at this moment,
Alone in the silence of dark night;
Where the history of the past is stretched in front of me,
Like a faraway whisper, faraway from the train which will not come back.
Of which sorrows shall I talk to you?
I am alone now,
Alone struggling with the shadow of loneliness,
Horrified by a crazy childish desire
Intended for those who are hidden behind the voice,
But the voice…
The voice steps forward,

(Becomes a strange warmth,
A tasty sea, as the size of the meaning that never appears,
As the depth of letters which are obliterated by the winter thunder).
Of which sorrows shall I talk to you?
I am a cursed letter,
A haunted letter;
The lost age is in search of me,
My body is in search of me,
And I in search of me.
For I am alone but not,
With people but not.
So leave me alone to sing the way I like.

ALI AL-SHARQAWI

The Grief of a Seagull [1]

So weary I am,
As though my soul is a languishing sparrow
Whose wings have been plucked.
So she wept blood,
And I wept, too, stealthily!
A sparrow…
As if enthralled by passion,
Flies towards me,
Speedily,
Ah, it falls, or about to fall…
But still tending to my direction.
It was only because hearts fly without wings
That she could fly towards me:
Wishing if love would fade away,
Wishing so.
But there are streams of absence between me and the dream
And the night is an enormous monster.
And the grave …is the gate.
Still the sparrow tumbles and tumbles,
Ah, what a prolonged torture.
Weariness, and a love- bearing twig is bent in the water.
Weariness. But my yearnings are unknown to others

Ah, what a yearning!
Distance kills me
But who knows that?
Who knows the streams carrying on their shoulders a gentle melody?
Who understands the star of eagerness shining from afar?
I am a withered flower shaken by dew drops,
Who can understand me?
Who?
I crave to embrace the voluptuous palm saplings,
But I am rejected,
I am a captured craver of signs.
Within me, the cloud tears me apart;
No words arrive to free me
Or to be carried by the echo
For waiting has wearied me,
Causing my heart to bleed and to bend
Like a dream,
Wandering from one land to another,
And I keep searching.
Ah, I am heart-broken.
A thread shines
Between my dream and ashes;
As if of pain I shine,
And see the sky
Not seen by others,
And watch dreaming stars blossom in madness,
And make rhymes one after another glitter.
Ah, Heaven manifests itself:

I behold breezes caressing the words passionately,
Breathing of hope.

And I smell the boisterous laughter of childhood
Overwhelm me with love,
And I run like an echo and shine…
Ah,
Like a blossomed nipple trembling on a wet breast,
The morning brightens,
My soul is ripped off passionately
Dispersing radiance.
Thus, blew the wind in bloom.
I gripped the sky's edges,
And cut off a wing from the cloud:
My imagination wept of love for my severed shoulder
And said: 'I need from the dream a scarf.'
I blew in it from the depth of my soul:
"to wake up" as a question.
His laughter rose,
My gaiety splintered,
And it began to dance
And rub the wound on my heart.

1. This is an example of Al-Sharqawi's early poetic achievement. The image of the seagull is skilfully woven around different colourful threads. The Shellean romantic tone of 'I fall upon the thorns of life! I bleed!' is resonant throughout the poem. Al-Sharqawi is also known for his daring and rather pictorial erotic images which are often employed to convey a political message.

IBRAHIM BU-HINDI

From a Lover …to the Sea

Restore my dream
And carry me on the blade of a traveller's oar
For my dream was
And still is
To forsake the moment of ecstasy,
And the two eyes
On whose eyelashes
I often venture.
Ah, if you take me as a wave, [**1**]
I will dance for light on the moon's face.
Ah, if you take me within you,
To the dreaming eyes
And weave me as sails
Where on her bosom I can sail,
And sing for the rain.
Ah, sea,
If I don't waste away in the moment of love,
I will see people like flowers,
Pouring scent on the ground,
Causing her sweet love to emerge.
So I can see the land full of peace
And love as a goddess
And child as a moon.

Ah, if age could draw me on your face
Like a migrant bird…
Restore my dream;
For the lover of the two eyes
Wont have pride
Today.

The Voice of an Imprisoned Lover

The past conceals itself behind the wind,
On its way is the atrocious past.
And through the wind, the intruders wish to repeat history with their hands.
They hide the lovers,
Let the jailer free
And imprison Lily's chant.

The past conceals itself in the lines of the lovers
And in the eyelashes of the lovers.
On its way is the atrocious past
Emerging from a direction chewed and thrown away by destiny.

My dear friends:
Still the roads are empty of lovers
Still the history of terror shines in the darkness of the night.
Belligerent Anushirwan firmly camps on our sea [**2**]
In his eyes 'Ahriman' glows
The atrocious past is on its way
To fight the befriended wind.

Raising our banner against the 'Ahriman',

We declare:

'Amwas' which sacrificed its eyes [**3**]

Rejects you as its lord,

It will break the siege of the plague.

1. The influence of the English Romantic poet Percy Shelley on modern Arab poets of the sixties and seventies was enormous. On the one hand, they shared his rebellious spirit and anti- conventionalist attitude to both religion and politics, and on the other hand, they embraced his subjectivity and egotistic outcry which is often represented by the use of apostrophe and invocations. This line is an echo of Shelley's:

> If I were a dead leaf thou mightiest bear
> If I were a swift cloud to fly with thee;
> A wave to pant beneath thy power, …

2. Anushirawan, or 'Chosroes' as he was called by the Romans, was one of the Sassanid kings in Persia whose empire reached South Arabia. Here, the poet refers to the deposed Shah of Iran who claimed that Bahrain was part of his kingdom. This allegation caused the fear of another Palestine, especially among Bahraini nationalists and Baathists.

2. In Zoroastrianism, it refers to the destructive Spirit or Satan

3. A village in Palestine. It was occupied by the Israelis in the 1967 war. The inhabitants were forced to leave for other towns in the West bank. Nevertheless, and despite Israeli's ethnic cleansing, the village still retained its old name. The poet draws a comparison between the threats and consequences of occupying Bahrain by the late Shah and the occupation of Amwas by the Israelis.

QASIM HADDAD

Portents

My mother's garment,
flapping on the aspiring roof
Of our house, [**1**]
Portends:
Sisyphus who once vanished
Has emerged.
Has emerged,
Carrying the rock of mankind. [**2**]
Ah, sea of ashes,
Sisyphus has emerged
And the free needs only gestures. [**3**]
On his forehead
There is the sign of a wounded yearning,
And in his hands
the veins weep over the crippled past,
A monotonous melody;
Sisyphus has emerged.
Pity on him.
He has emerged
Dragging his pale long years
Over the aspiring roof of our house
And from the minaret.

Hasan Marhamah

O, my mother's embroidered garment, [4]
Was that a loss!?
I wish I had accompanied him on a trip
The benefit of it would be without loss.

***

From a palm leaf
Stirred by the waves on the beach,
From a little girl dancing with a rope,
From the echo of sweet melody,
Rises the dawn of good omens.
Rises to kill melancholy and autumn.
So welcome to a thousand Sisyphoi
To occupy the house,
To conquer the night's seas
And to wreck the wall-rats' fortresses.
Our island has wept enough
Has had misery enough
The bereaved ode should cease,
And the song of mankind,
Of tomorrow and construction
Should start.
Never dies
The night in our depths,
Never;
For the dawn roars in its hands…
A light tears our dirty thick garment:
It is a new light.
Oh, my mother's garment fluttering in the clouds:

Tear away the curtain of silence,
Sweep the fogs,
And ring out with your sound the sleepy ones;
The day has come,
Break our frost and in return
We offer you our good omens.
Oh, my mother's garment…
The candles won't fade away,
The black rock may be softened
The ribs pain may be softened
And there will be love of mankind cheering
Within us.
Scaring the autumn of our world:
The mankind candle will care for us.
Sisyphus has come to spread my mother's garment
And continue the melody,
So rejoice,
Oh garment,
Announce to the sun
The death of the dark cloud
And the death of our sins.

There will be another day
To complete the human journey,
To weave our green dawn,
And to forget our sorrows.
Oh, our destination is too far…
But we will reach it;

For Sisyphus' echo calls us.
We will sail
Despite the chains on our feet and hands.

Ah, Sisyphus,
Like you
We will join daytime,
Will dive in the heart of the seas,
Penetrate the heart of the night...
The heart of impossibility,
And carry mankind
And burn on our shores
The sea-dogs and sorrows. [**5**]
Tomorrow
We will depart,
Tomorrow
We will depart,
Tomorrow
We will sail to the sea of the night
On a dhow and palanquin.
Tomorrow we will depart,
Oh, mother,
And revive the tales of the sailor
Once again...

The Entry to the Entrance

I gave my hand the sweet thing [**6**]
And I remembered
Remembered the beginning
The step in colour and the universe
Remembered the sea as a red woman
Remembered the water which screamed at me
Enter
And I entered
Entered the mirrors of dreams

And I was the greeting of the past for the new arrival
I saw things teaching me
I spoke to the running possibility
I said
I will know
The feather said I knew
So I came crossed the Hell of the universe and Paradise
Probed the future
Sat in the lounge of nonsense
And remembered the first mirror screaming at me
Enter
And I entered
Became a gleam
And spoke the language of water
I saw the feather falling from my body and my hand speak
I spoke
I saw a god is born in the mirror of people
So I filled the cup…

Hasan Marhamah

Secrets

I see in a woman a mirror revealing a secret
And reconciling conspiracies
I marry her
We will dress and will erase our steps
I stare at her
And she stares at me
We don't believe in our secrets
Because after the evening
The armies launch their attack
And the kings blame their countrymen

The Fifth Attempt/Text

The white page is [7]
The lady of speech
And the slave of the readers
It is white after being written
And remains white

Creation

This earth is vibrating [8]
Where shall I place my feet?

The Season of a Dream

Pity on me
You, the fourth impossibility
And be fulfilled.

The Captain

He invented a ship and made it towers for banners to rejoice.
And fenced the water with a seal of minarets. Only the sea-gulls
Knew the light and the wide orbits.
He filled the lanes with wine and bread and loosened the stairs
For the coming sailors. He built castles whose whiteness filled
The space of the horizon.
And stood like a tall mast, watching and waiting for sailors.
He was late. Too late.
But he stood waiting.

The Horses

Thus the horses gallop thrusting the tobacco carts and sweeping the tranquillity
Of the *suq*
Questioning the women on the errors of the night and revealing to them the secrets
Of disgrace and the fervour of embers.
Wild horses, loaded with the fountains' ecstasy, penetrate the evening tales
To seduce
The quarry: the delight of the sin,

Hasan Marhamah

The limbs: the radiance of the body,

The horses have the tradition of hoopoes and the unruliness of horns;

They are welcomed by the church addicts and beggars as a sign of retribution.

And when the attack rinses the rattle of the beer glass, the horses settle in the terrace of the bars,

Leaving the women to hug freely and breed a generation of combative

Tyrants.

1. The hanging of clothes on the roof is a sign of the arrival of a relative or close member of the family.
2. The ill-treated and disgruntled sea- divers are compared to the Greek hero, Sisyphus, who is the symbol of defiance and sacrifice.

3. This is the second part of a line by the well-known Arab poet Abu Taiyib Al-Mutanabbi (915-965) which reads:
'The slave learns by force while gestures will suffice for the free'. The English equivalent is : 'A word to the wise is enough'. The poet here argues that all signs indicate that victory is imminent.

4. It was customary to hang new and coloured clothes on the roof of a house to announce the arrival of a dear one.

5. 'Sea-dogs' in this line does not refer to the gentle sea creatures that environmentalists and all animal lovers wish to preserve. Here it connotes tyrants and traitors.

6. The poem is a vivid manifestation of space as an active poetic entity. Qasim Haddad brilliantly and effectively splashes as an impeccable artist, on the white page, his poetic thoughts and speculations to create prismatic and palpable shapes and the forms of spatial images.

7. What a remarkable poetic and personality transformation Qasim Haddad has undergone recently! From an uncompromising revolutionary in the first three of his collections to a bard in quest of perfection and ultimate truth in his later works. While

other Bahraini political poets were deeply immersed in surrealistic and abstract images after the political reforms of 2001, Qasim Haddad resorted to form innovations and techniques. The political tone of his early poems was transferred into an amalgam of novel poetic shapes and styles as his adoption of haiku poetic forms shows.

8. This is an example of Qasim Haddad's excellent creation of a single concrete image by manipulating concise words which is reminiscent of Ezra Pound's '*In a Station of the Metro*'.

SAEED AL-OWEINATI

The Demise of the Palm-tree Era

"Ah, time ...Ah time
Even these palm-trees have turned withered...
No longer have they any traces on the great land of Delmon..." [**1**]

Ah, legendary palm-tree
Wake up...
And remember the irrigation time,
The names of the men in farms,
The sailors, the hands,
The dreams of the village youth,
And the dark colour of the dawn,
When the village earth trembled,
And burst in bounteousness and anger.[**2**]
And remember the colour of your date clusters
And the quivering of your leaf,
When we watched you as a hut
Built by the villagers from leaves;
Then you became ropes,
And songs in the merry time of harvest,
And roots watered by the sweat of the forefathers,
And the night wrapped in a mantle.

* * *

You, the palm tree of my land,
Time has abandoned you,
The dark forces have stabbed you [**3**]
So has the plague of agony
And now you are naked;
The strangers, who became the gentlemen of our era, longed for your slaughter;
Blinded by the glitter of barren gold in the world of darkness,
They set you on fire.

You, legendary palm-tree of my land,
Do you recall the tales of joy planted in your soil,
While the hands of the village youths
Trembled on the days of generosity
And the celebrations of Hussein...? [**4**]
Do you recall the village youths
Docking the marsh roots
Before the next harvest
And before the cultivation,
So the depths of the villages
Become the cradle of fertility
And the birth of richness?
Do you recall the boys' circumcision,
And the times of prosperity,
Which triggered to your mind the silent scene
Of the villagers' murmurs on their way
To wash near the pool. [**5**]

* * *

You , palm tree of my land,
You are the crescent and the moonlit nights;
We played under your trees in childhood.

On our faces was the colour of joy,
You were the fields and the nights of harvest.
So the joy will be complete in your eyes,
When the nights arrive and grandmothers narrate past stories
And our fathers, watching the stars, never slumber in the quiet night,
The mothers' kindness filling us with warmth in a wintry night.
The roses' hearts float in every farm
Like a star shining in our neighbourhood,
Knocking on the door every morning
To sing with the purl of water its rhythm
And sweetens the ears at the time of meeting.

Ah , legendary palm-tree of my land,
Wake up:
We have become strangers,
And the sea has become the source of misery,
And the world a confrontation.
You, the beautiful legendary palm-tree,
Do you recall my father
Among the clusters of palm-dates
And my brother farmer near the stream
Singing melodies to your morning
While the youths of our village

Spreading the palm-balms
And plies of palm-leaves at night?
Do you recall the cock's crow
And the purl of water,
The sweet wedding ritual
And your relatives
Who began the ceremonies?

* * *

You, the palm tree of my land,
Now, they have forgotten you [**6**]
And tomorrow their world will become a legend,
Houses of stone
And will be ravaged by the strangers' hands,
Your roots will be devoured by the hounds
And you will be straight away blamed for.
And now they share among themselves
The moments of disgrace and the stigma of memories,
By betrothing you to Death,
Perhaps the clay of the grave is better… [7]

You, the palm-tree of my land,
Tomorrow heralds victory,
Then, they will be cursed by all the sparrows of my homeland,
By the sea-gulls, the fish, the shade and the past memories.
Tomorrow we will curse them,
So will the craftsmen of this world.

Hasan Marhamah

Ah, palm-tree,
For your sake I wait for that moment,
For the rise of the dawn,
For the emergence of warm-water roses,
The smiles of children;
For the dispersion of the clouds,
The vanishing of melancholy
And the return of the land
Like the sun with a birth.

1. Delmon is a Sumerian name given to Bahrain islands. It meant 'the land of holy gods' where the epic of Gilgamesh was originated.

2. The two words 'trembling' and 'exploding' refer to the festivities and the high spirit of the villagers.

3. Literally 'dark forces' refers to what is known in Islamic history as 'Black Apostasy' which was the defection of some tribes in the Arabian Peninsula from Islam after the demise of Prophet Mohammad.

4. Refers to the fourth Shia Imam, Husain Bin Ali and his anniversaries.

5. Bahrain was known for its natural pools and streams. The most notable ones were Adhari, Qasari ,Um Mushoom , El-hanainiya, El-raha. Except for Adhari which has become a pubic park, the others have either dried out or have been transferred into commercial public places.

6. "They" refers to the villagers.

7. Al-Oweinati here draws an apocalyptic vision of the destruction of the village.

YAQOOB AL-MUHARRAQI

A Solo on Mayakovski's Guitar

In a public area-

Mayakovski: "I don't know what has happened to my throat, I shall stop reciting my poems to the audience. Perhaps this is my last night."

To loneliness,

Revolution has captured me with a swarm of surprising colours,

I was the exile, carrying within my heart

The lark of imprisoned anger.

I called my exiled comrades;

We danced.. the beer-taste drew blue circles on the two eyes.

My destination is the cities which wake up in violent lightening

And sleep on the rhythm of water,

Like a mirror cracked by grief

And shores on which rotten fish are thrown.

My destination is forests of snow

-Can roads take us there?-

"I walk a long distance on a street,

Inattentive of my whereabouts like dissolved fire."

Shall I sit on the memory of usurped islands

Where only the jailer's keys separate me from the earth's joy?
The jailer's keys attach me to the earth's joy;
I feel exile in the eye of the dead fish migrating to the vast river.

(There dwells a woman in the bottom, writing to the children of the vast river, since she was born in June. As the tide carries her, she sings:

To die in this world is easy but to lead a life is more difficult.")

In the tavern, we shake our heads,
Alone you rise;
Love poems are visible in your pocket.
In the tavern, the cup falls
(a mistress emerges from the bottom of the cup;
There is a bomb on the map of time
Breathing the names of the martyrs) [**1**]
You, the lark of anger in my imprisoned chest,
Be transformed into a red lark,
Between thunder and fear,
And behind the palm tree's conscience.

In one of the public areas-

In protest to an error which happens in the world...
Mayakovski is hanged while holding his guitar.

1. This is an allusion to the death of Mohamad Bu Nafoor, a political activist and a member of Bahrain Liberation Front (renamed: the National Democratic Action Society) who died in a mysterious explosion on 2 August 1973. At around 10 o'clock night, a bomb blast shattered his house which was located in the poor Hala district in Al-Muharraq and caused his death instantly.

IMAN ASSIRI

A Dream [1]

As though sitting on a throne pulsating, I observe the Caesars devouring this poor blood; thus I grab my cup and drink to the health of the prisoners and cheer up since starvation is a hostage of the United Nation's decision.

As though sitting…I see them planting us in small piles where scabby woodworm lives, feeds melancholy and sad gazes. And we bathe and blossom, and

forget that we, like rinds, bend inside the shells as we are shaken.

As though sitting on the throne, you see me full of joy, swaying the child and dream of the green rug,

And glance at the coming caravans loaded with milk in the horizon,

And I ask:

Do I have a share of the milk?

They reply: after the conference.

My sight exhausted me, my child slept … and the caravans unloaded near my door…I ran in the desert in search of a water well…

A stone cracked under my feet,

That moment I realized that I had a little nap.

It's Me, a Skylark [2]

To observe a decayed wall,
And to enter it heedlessly;
A shaking wall,
I clasp it with my feet.
To be cushioned by you tonight,
To be rescued, to be feared so that my gown protects me,
To fidget in my chair,
Stipulating a profit … and a dagger … for a share,
    My yawing glows with arms,
    For sleep passes swiftly between the eyelid and the time of salvation.
I enter, shame is shaken,
Injects in you blood to be congested in veins heedless of cleanliness.
    I enter myself;
    A storm embraces me,
    Emits atoms to transfer me into an eagle,
    And the rain becomes an obituary,
    Over my terraced forehead
    Whilst I pity the debtor's book,
    The prayers of the current debts respond.
I dance,
A frenzied dance, which make a child smile.
Over the children's imaginary throne,
I continue pulsating, my eyelid is burnt.
I grab the square throne

to stretch… but it tumbles down.
The skylark remains a shade for the child, a witness
Who can see the acts of centuries in the roots,
And in the disguised trunk that fell,
I dance successively,
I turn, contact successively,
Turn…,
It's me, a skylark.

On the Terrace

On the Terrace,
Sprinkled with dewdrops and surprises,
Pages of disgusting newspapers
Are stunned to see
Dewdrops fall on their black- coated letters.
On the terrace,
A starving cat with a swelling dust-covered skeleton entered,
On the terrace,
The she cat crouched, moaning, and moaning.
Her moans grieved and coloured the desolate villages and orchards
Like the jubilation of the sun at noon
On the terrace.
Surprises continued
As long as dewdrops accompanied the earth.

1. Iman Assiri is one of the pioneers of prose poetry in Bahrain. Virtually all poetic devices are observed in her prose poems. Furthermore, they are characterized by a flow of surrealistic imageries often fused with humour and cynicism.

2. In addition to being a well-known woman poet, Iman Assiri is also a connoisseur of painting. In her poetry, the fusion of colours is brilliantly employed to produce various political and social images.

SALMAN AL-HAYKI

The Tunnel of Ashes [1]

(For Flower and Others)

They advanced against you:
First, the ash-coloured sea,
And the waves of the crushing sands.
They drove forward,
Struck,
And withdrew…
Then your disfigured face was inflected with the zoom of domestic eyes
And heaps of fresh flesh which
Tinged the apparel of the flowers, meteors and the withered branches.
Flowed out, unknowingly, across the caravans or the eyes of the passers-by;
Heaps of fresh flesh.
They drove forward,
Struck,
And withdrew…
And behind the debris, our palm-trees wept
And with the fire the sunset pillars purified themselves,
The suns vanished…
The sea wave ripped apart the top of the nectar and the smoke.
Hence, a flower emerged.

Its wounded bird was overfilled with throbbing
Until it dwindled behind the immolation water and the dreams of time.
Their caravans returned to us…
The crooked brows smeared with ashes came back to us,
Times came back through the waist of a thin camel,
Through the blowing of the wind, came back the country's caravan.
There, you will one day see the passengers,
Dragging behind them their dough
And staring through the valleys of murmur…
To prepare a bread from a tender sun
And in their heavy loincloths lies a bitter wound;
A flower on a small twitch
Overfilled with nectar
Composed as in labour among the branches
And as in the comfort of childbirth.
Whiteness sat dressing the pure palm cheek
And through dough-like night appears a ray
And a hiss is spread in the night's rustling.
A flower on a small twitch
With evaporated nectar
Sobs like a rose when abandoned by dew drops
And in her eye there lies a buried sadness.
Their caravans came back to us;
The whole company returned from the dawn,
Filled with longing towards longing
And evening arrived in colour
But daytime in torture.
Tears of fire merge into the tree's chest,

And the flower is parched with thirst.
She drinks volcano water and
The apple rose
But she does not flash
Or burst.
There, they have come back to us…

There, they have stormed the rocks and have come back to us;
They shed the valleys lemon and came back,
They dispersed all the stars on the roads and came back.
And a flower emerged,
Following her the wave voluntarily
While the night death-rattle preceded her
And her face disappeared amongst the walls of echo and jasmine,
Yet engraved in the memory of time!

1- What characterizes Al-Hayaki's poetry is tremendous linguistic capabilities to convey profound and impregnated revolutionary images in an impersonal note. In this poem, the rhetoric of inevitable victory (as in almost all Marxist poetry) is portrayed in a series of conflicts and confrontations which carry an enormous emotional weight and are expressed in powerful symbolic language.

FATHIYA Al-AJLAN

Waiting

I hid your eyes within my ribs and skin [**1**]
And left behind a country which does not carry a name
Or people or trees.
At night,
I unfolded my ribs and let you out.

I entertained your eyes,
Danced in your clothes at the weddings,
Kissed with love the fingers of your palm,
And planted flowers.
For here the land is barren,
But my love will irrigate your heart,
It will make it a garden for sparrows,
And I will build bridges and seas so we can cross with yearnings.

In my arms the sleeping child
Was your love,
The blossomed flowers were your love
The dreaming lawn was your heart
Where were your eyes?
I knew them in the entire world,
They declared something
They declared
They....

I was embracing your belongings,
Waiting for someone to knock on the door,
And receive your papers.
So I can weep,
And dance with children.
I hid you in my life for years
And I slept without life many times.
For I know my life is a deadly wilderness. [**2**]
Within my ribs I hid you.
Will you enter my skin in celebrations? [**3**]

Childhood

The more you stretch your hands
The longer stays the mirage.
I laugh and cry,
And cover my face.
Can you provide me with another palm?

A Wave

Like the circulation of melody,
Your love is engraved on my heart;
As it melts away,
I fly towards you like the rotation of pain.

The Wanderings of Scheherazade

I am Scheherazade and you are the night whose whisper is like madness. [4]

I am Scheherazade and my tears are your eyes hidden by the eyelids.

So keep silent.

For in my heart's beating,

There is a story before the sunrise.

So keep silent and talk to me in your silence;

Perhaps silence is the passing key.

I am Scheherazade and my story is the stars' dream.

1. The imagery of the rib as a symbol of creation occurs in both Judaism and Christianity in relation to the creation of Eve from Adam's crooked rib, though it is not stated in the Holy Quran . In the Sumerian mythology of the god Enki, however, the rib symbolized healing and prosperity. Here, Fathiya Al-Ajlan implies that there is no safer place to protect a dear one than keeping him within the rib which is so close to the heart.

2. The pain of loneliness and the hopelessness of waiting have transformed her into a wilderness.

3. Because of bareness, the ribs can no longer protect her love so she wants him to live within her skin at the time of celebrations, which literally means when he returns home.

4. The queen narrator in *Tales of the Arabian Nights* (One Thousand and One Nights). She narrates to the blood-thirsty king Schehreyar a tale every night to postpone her inevitable execution.

NABEELA ZUBARI *

I Feel You [1]

As a lamp-light's caress of a place,
And a morning's longing for joy in harbours;
As a script no longer in need of words,
And as a life-giving sip to quench the thirsty universe.

I feel you,
Whilst sitting amidst the cities of prayers,
Tampering with silence,
Re-arranging the order of time in your papers,
Concealing some love,
Or all love…
In the pool of your eye
Or locking up thousands of empty wardrobes,
Except the one with my picture;
You will then rummage through the whiteness and the ground,
And the busy horizon with the nightingale's thirst,
Perhaps to find me:
As a phantom making up for the of cruelty of distance
And consenting to your kindness.

I feel you
Amongst the fear of the lost gardens,
As a brook sought by my life,
So it glittered with the water flow
Amidst the anticipation of the palm trees
And the alienation of basil and henna leaves.
It glittered with it:
The dewdrops purified my brow
And I am back to my place
So that time looms through my face
And I can see you without my eyes,
And I feel you.
Feel you outside the forest fences
Dozing with lilies in my palms.

I feel you
Whenever daytime turns verdant
And the angels repose.
I feel you amidst the island of pulsation
And the flow of yearnings.
Come forward, then, despite the distance,
Come closer to me.

Hasan Marhamah

Distance

The roads seemed scraps of paper,
Lanes were like evaporated moans
And the nymphs were like foggy clouds.
Where has life disappeared?

Or where shall we find it?
For there is no road with an end…
All the labyrinths fill the hearts with alienation.
This road is a torn book
Whose addresses are lost,
And it will never come back.
All directions look like prisons and blockades,
And compasses are the signs of loss and suffering.
Is death, therefore, approaching?
Or is it the sea- breeze, encircling the whirl wind, which directs us?
Or the pomegranate's scent concealed in the caves of fountains?
Or is it a dove on a tall roof
Whose gates look mirage-like helmet!?
No, the road never returns,
Never returns…
Ah life,
I am lost in your space.

How Can I Close the Gate of Life ...Without You?

Because I am used to ...
Watching you
Wake up every morning
On your own...
Attending to the lilies of joy
With your breath...

Because I am used to
Watching you
Hide my dream in your palm...
And dissolve palaces under my feet...
Then, sparkle like a star
In a moon-lit horizon! [**2**]

Because I am used to
Sipping your voice in my morning
And walking on a melody sung in all parts of my body
Every day...
So how can I close the gate of life without you?
How can I survive an era without your eyes?
Or breathe a fragrance without your trace...?
So will you be blessed with a horizon
Without my singing pulses...?
And will you travel alone...
Alone...
Without me?!!

* Nabeela Zubari's poetry is closely associated with her active involvement in social and literary activities and in particular women's campaigns for equal rights. Her academic career as an Educational Technology professor has given her the ability and skill to recapture vivid pictorial imageries often enveloped in sensual veins. In these three poems, Nabeela Zubari treats the theme of love, in its pure and unadulterated forms, exploring the relationship of a woman with a man and celebrating the ecstasy of the unity of soul and body. She may be, to some extent, indifferent to the social issues that most women poets in Bahrain and the Arab world are involved in, however, her simple diction, absorbable poetic images and engrossment in human relationships are indeed, praiseworthy. In fact, they represent the fragility and vulnerability of women. Furthermore, they flow spontaneously and innocently, heedless of any social or religious barriers. It is a revelation of the woman's sincere feelings and steadfastness.

1. One of the salient themes in Nabeela Zubari's poetry is the pain of separation, whether physical or emotional, between the two lovers which is conducive to a state of total desperation and frustration.

2. Literally means 'in the horizon that washes away the darkness of the night with the moon-light.'

AHMAD MADAN

The Morning of Writings and Roads [1]

There is a fault in our seasons: This sacrosanct serenity, like our slumber, Reaps a soul in our lines, tracks us…

Does the body greet me,
Like the awakening of flame,
Or the extinguishing of drowsiness?
Does it greet this respectful audience?
And my face,
And drowns me with his diffused details?
I shall snatch the untouched clock from the moment of surprise,
For mornings are void
And anxiety kindles my door,
Spurts out dew drops
At my two cheeks and this pillow.
My soul's cloud pours
A drop...
A drop...
A fiery drop.

Hasan Marhamah

Over me the tree of yearnings
Writes this ode:
Here is our branch,
Plants a sign around us
So we can learn how to fly?!

The roads perish
with passers-by
As blocks of smoke
And stone caress the surface of my footsteps
And the shade like the warmth of embrace,
Ascends the stairs of ecstatic feet
Where songs of the sands rise.
So does the women's swing
as in our state of intoxication.
The pupils begin from here,
Composing poetry.
There is a secret in this space;
Bags carry bread and dreams
Inaugurate this whiteness.

My craving is like a lord,
And I am as a necessity located in the heart of this passion.
How many times have I been dissected by a road and a morning
And thrown on the threshold of the city?
Is there a space here
or lines?!

Words pass gently over his body,
Does he realize its solace was
letters
And in his hands fall the sparrows of this cry
Or was it the pride of childhood and primary books?

A sign covers the distance of the pavements,
Shelters its postings,
But made wet by the rain and dust.
It relieves it from the men's chatter with a greeting;
The men probe the surface of the dew,
Harvest the daytime
And the whole distance collapses.
They are the outcome of tiredness,
And the absence of astonishment
And the shine of the morning

Does the edge of the writing talk to me?!
Or revise me with a page of paper!!!

Hasan Marhamah

1. One of the reasons for ambiguity and, to some extent, confusion in Ahmad Madan's early poetry, as is vivid in the this poem, is the fact that his poetic imageries lack correlative support. They neither allude to any social or political events as in the poetry of his contemporaries, nor based on subjectivity and impersonal notes. However, his profession as an architect has assisted him a lot in shaping the aesthetics of his poetry. His experiment with concrete or visual poems is, indeed, a sign of development in Contemporary Bahraini poetry.

FAWZIA AL-SINDI *

When the Homeland Blossoms in the Heart

My love,

You are the thorny rose grown in my heart,
In a night where grief learns a craft,
When homeland learns the craft of how to play melodies on dead bodies
Where the dust of sorrow bleeds on my body.
You are the tattoo
Engraved like a fertility god on blood.

My homeland,

This thirsty and pregnant land,
Like a seal on the tail of the present rulers
Is called my homeland.
Can astonishment be kindled in the magical lyrics of this *mawwal* [**1**]
Which is the warmth of gatherings?
Can astonishment be kindled?
My lover's face is a panting dream,
A passion traversing the alleys of horrifying fantasy,
In quest of a time bearing a river of blood ,
Of a god endowing on the thirsty tree the warmth of cloud,

Of a warmth extending to embrace lovers
In a country where thugs
Assassinate the yearnings of poets for trivial matters.

My love,

My voice will emerge from behind the debris of the universe,
From a country rolling in the memory of the sun,
And in the eyes of a child.
Will emerge
To restore to the sea its holiness,
To love its purity,
And to glorify the epic of love forgotten under the clerics' gowns.

My homeland,

You are the wound spread from my heart to the labyrinth of letters,
You are the bridge built by chained hands that have grown old,
But still a shackle to light the homeland's eyes.

My homeland,

I carry my grief as a candlestick in the silence of lonely nights;
My sign is a chisel of desire,
My blood still flows to sketch in your eyes the face of my beloved and the sun,
It falls to blossom in my heart.

My love,

Will the exiled light come to you tomorrow
In a night where crime is committed
And in a homeland where somnolence is celebrated?
Will the light come?

The Soul Asylum (Fragment)

Less laborious
Appears the distance towards you,
As though it passes through my descent,
Towards a door tracking
Two feet tumbling over the pebbles endlessly.

Squatting in a night cellar,
Acquainted with the cell of passions,
Sown as wheat surrendering to the rugged scythe with a stranger's joy,
Numbed with wounds and the pain of shanks,
Like the flow of a spear he takes refuge in me.

Had not been for you,
I would not have faded away,
Embracing all this air.
I would not have been cast in a hollow
Spinning the sands' heedlessness
For the wretchedness of its desire.

Hasan Marhamah

I call you in my name
Positioning myself in your throne of blood,
With letters which will sob the doubt of my blood.

I call you in my name:
Either to win or to lose,
Amongst the limbs and the wounds.

I will put off this vacuum as a burden
deserted by our vow.
So bring closer the mirror of your daring glow
So I can be the quakes of the pebbles.

* Fawzia Al-Sindi is, indubitably, one of the most talented woman poets in Bahrain, a poet of great poetic vision and sensitivity. However, her disregard of or rather negligence towards the necessity of adopting a poetic form – a pattern – a poetic form discipline– has seriously undermined her poetry. A careful look at her poetry from the earliest one *Awakening* from where the above poem has been extracted to the latest collection entitled *The Soul Asylum* (a fragment is included here), exhibits an unrestrained flow of ideas, emotions and imageries, which run indefinitely like a wild furious animal. Consequently, her poems appear diffused with unintelligible ideas and images which surpass the capacity or space of the text. This technique may work in poetry recitations where reading improvisation often accompanies the text.

1. A colloquial folk song often sung by the sea divers on the board of a dhow.

AHMAD AL-AJAMI *

Day of Reckoning

Unbearable is to me a kingdom devoid of rivers. In the golden beaks of sparrows, the rocks are invigorated to build a fountain and poetry, and a white sky for me to write on it. My joy is a broken carriage and a noon with the maturity of elephants. My wife resembles me in language and in gathering the angels at night. The letters, planted for the remaining hollow butterflies, rise. This wild wound destroys the garden, and the war stiffens the lark's wings. In my countenance, the climate forest turns yellow, the light is darkened in the grave-like cups of which I drank and died and in my arms was a sunken forest.

The Lamp's Vision

It sways on the dead bodies, the day's smell is like a mysterious growling, has rainbow-like interjections attached to the swollen bodies, similar to the chilliness of hearts. It remains in its sway and rises like the grief of homelands. The serenity of treason is never extinguished from its light.

Hasan Marhamah

Necessity

Do you remember how we met?
And how dewdrops sprang up?
We were gathered up in an intoxicated bottle,
Undressing our limbs from their paradise,
Letting our hearts run on the night windows.
How beautiful we were
As we freed the air with a confused smile?
I listened to the tremble of coincidence
And you were attentive to the *howdah* of desires! [**1**]
Incidentally, what did the rain mean by mentioning us?

Wound

I laugh hilariously
Whenever we sit together,
This has been observed by the sky
Always
But
When a woman confronts me
Or caresses me a cold bed,
My tears overflow
Over my chest.
I don't know where they spring from.

* Ahmad Al-Ajami's skill in successfully casting his words and images into well-presented patterns which are less metaphorical or symbolic is praiseworthy. The brevity and conciseness of his images accord brilliantly with the erotic themes that often permeate his poems.

1. Literally it means a 'palanquin' or a 'canopied seat fitted on the back of a camel' more often used by women. Here it means the peak or the climax of desires.

KARIM REDHI

A Child's Lament

To Belief and Disbelief,
To the sea similar to God's wonder before the Creation,
To the cities stained with reading and vigilance,
To the two rising hands from milk and liquor,
To the hallucinating lands in sleep,
Calling the names of the victims
Packing in the bags their flesh
And dispensing the gentle blood
To the airports.
To the growling wind in a clay pot,
To the sad dog,
To the girls whose fingers are embedded in oil and henna,
To the virgin who has embraced her books and slept
In the barns of the moon:
A child dies today
His pocket is full of paper and sweets.
He was dreaming before the words rose
From his dictionary
And before he rearranges
The pictures.

The Crow's Repentance

We will repent of the crow's croak,
And of satirizing the city.
We will repent of the furnished rooms
With piles of battles and poems
And the valuable documents:
Our finger prints and the undertakings of the losers are for you,
For you are also the bowels of the bags
Exchanged in sober transactions.
We will repent of our old dogmas
And will be satisfied with less uttering words,
With a strap of jasmine, leaving behind the paradise we dreamed of.
We will resort to our indecent beds,
Crammed with pale women;
Mothers of some children whose fingers blemish our beards
In the serenity of daytime.
We will say:
We have repented and it is over
And banishments no longer favour our cries.
We have repented,
So take us back to the forgotten land,
On the deck of a ship.
To the homeland which will reject us if we returned,
Will send us on exile but still we love it,
It will send us to exile but banishments no longer favour our cries.

1. Karim Rehdi's style is lucid and non-propagandist, even though he writes political poems. The themes of exile and homeland are depicted with utmost scrutiny and care in a melodious and lyrical form. His poetry is often imbued with a cynical note.

JAFFAR AL-JAMRI

Not Deliberately Resorting to Rhythm

I often resort to rhythm deliberately,
So that I remember that on its borders I am some of its metaphors...
I imagine a woman there...
There, in the coffee-shop serving during the extra time,
Which is a burden already ceased,
Since she joined the coffee shop there...
Why then, whenever did the birds of her presence fly away,
The space was affected,
And I no longer could waive to the clouds?
Oh, my unbearable guest
Enough recklessness like a horse at twenty,
This will cease when you appear
Carrying your eternal sleep.
The coffee shop would not wail if the girl abandoned her attractions...
But if you don't turn up, it will be pure falsehood.
So get up to curse the things:
The erect fence and the fortune-teller's device.
There , in that far away coffee shop,
Time appears like a broken violin,
And a flute in its secret hallucination.
I don't often resort to rhythm
But experiment is its absurdist lesson.

And I did not regret my mistakes
But they pitied me on my regrets.

Guarding the Past

To retrieve Time from the moment of conception is to abbreviate or delete human history and his presence and achievements since his creation on this planet. It is an abbreviation and deletion which announces whatever they wish, consciously or unconsciously- what is counted as an achievement will remain "transitory" for he is the "inhabitant" and the generator.. What is counted, remains stable but mobile at the level of effects and addition... What is counted is to be the receiver, the follower and the obedient one, and he must be so. Like a vision that some of its advocates affirm it. . that the past which lies within that vision, is the only absolute authority... which deepens the justifications and establishes some kind of "guard" on the past in fear of the release of the present and its future issues!

1. In his early poems, Al-Jamri's poetry suffered from obscurity and confusion as a result of his use of far-fetched images and disassociated chains of vocabulary. However, since his return from the UAE, where he worked there for years, his voice has been consolidated firmly in the poetic developments in Bahrain.

FATIMA TAITOON

A White Man [1]

There was a white man in the dark,
Who never vanished or moved forward,
So we thought he was in the last dregs of his age
Hallucinating.

****

We did not reject sweetness until we reached ecstasy,
And neither did spring from our hands lotus leaves.
Within our eyes lies a yellow evening
And within our eyebrows glitters the moon.

If we miss the promise of a tanned rhyme,
And a restless patience,
If we roam on the departing guitar,
When the heart's pulses diminish,
And time augments in dejection.
If the frenzy of festivities fall into slumber
And the brook is left unattended,
And the morning sinks,
If we were not there...

****

Hasan Marhamah

There stands a white man in the Eid garlands,
Between a rock and a shining shell;
Evening wears out and convulses in the intoxication of death,
And rolls in the hours of sunset;
The whisper of pain arrives,
Hisses in the chest and howls in the Moments…
Who is that white man
Shining like the sun?
His eyes have drowned in expectations
And touched the prime of the wind.

****

Not in the whiteness of the light
Did he drown in fear
Or on his way back from a frolic wintry night.

(Neither his face ceased from whiteness
Nor did he creep to the treasures)

****

Standing in the wakefulness of the green sun,
Crying in a pure whisper,
Passing within the footsteps,
He is similar to the white man;
This white man.
And the universe is in prayer.

Tonight is Our Celebration [2]

In a similar night we were,
As Death was mine the night before,
Where I fulfilled the painful paths,
And longed for the harbour and the demolished ships.
Darkness contained me,
And on the spring of the evening I bled.
Tonight, was our celebration,
So we were united in silence.
Some palm leaves swayed
And hastened the cluster of grapes,
Neither a strange boy
Nor a strange girl
Filled the cups…
They did not water the lily tonight,
The heart leapt and reddened the grapes,
The dagger inhaled
And the giant played his game tonight ever,
I am covered with the blankets of fire,
But appear nude to the Word,
As you are to the sun.
Wish you were pleased
Like your pleasure for honey…for a kiss.
There in the travels of love,
My blood coloured my first night,
And in narration my heart sought refuge.
History belongs to you,

Or perhaps, you, to the sun.

Ah, Words, you have purified me from the sun,

Ah, candlesticks,

Sanctuary,

Cruel night,

My tears for your sake have dried up…

And you have never…! [**3**]

1. In a series of astounding symphonic stanzas, Fatima Al-Taitoon displays variegated imageries spatially woven within the framework of the poem. The hanging or, in fact, the entangling of the white man in the web of nowhere, makes him neither a reality nor an apparition. The white man may not exist but ironically he is embedded within the whiteness of the text surrounded by dazzling colours.

2. Fatima Al-Taitoon celebrates the moments of poetic creation, the descent of the Muse in this poem. These are the moments of great emotional as well as imaginative surge, totally unrestrained, uncontrollable and unpredictable.

3. Fatima Al-Taitoon's poetry is characterized by mystery. It is like probing into a deep hollow cave, with voices and images surrounding you. The endings, interestingly enough are mysterious too.

IBRAHIM SHABAAN

O, Abel's Sister [1]

Still reciting the Sura of disobedience, [2]
Crossing to the following era,
And beginning from the end.
I still embrace the kindness of all those
Who came,
And stayed in front of me.
I had not tasted the slumber of delusions,
Since I joined the chorus of priests.
Whoever reveals the earth's Book to the kingdom,
Closes with discretion the gates of Heaven
And humanizes the renewed science to mankind.

Ah, Heart, do not conceal yourself from me;
Here, kinship shows no mercy
And asleep are all the invisible people. [3]
Over the waves of darkness,
Ah, Abel's Sister,
Spread all the rules;
Neither the inspirer has won
Nor the intellect has entered here
Within time or space,
Since Sumar 'ha hana' or 'enki' [4]

Who sold water to humanity
And kept huge amounts of soil
In the womb of smoke.

I will not appeal today for commandments,
I will not live without a vision,
Without an address.
I will not be driven towards disgrace,
From the tomb of silence:
For some living is worse than non-living.
All armies passed here
Unaware of the rising sword of people.
And I,
I cry for the enthusiasm of my bereaved folks
And complain of my destiny.
Ah, goddess of free men,
No longer are the palm trees here rebellious,
But are in accord with people without principles.
Ah, Abel's sister, be a witness:
I have lost hope in the complaint,
My wounded words moan;
There is no glow in front of me,
And no one is there to face my sword.

Woe to the people who still fear the night,
Long for the wind for safety
Pay homage to the Torah to kill peace. **[5]**
Millions of years have passed

And the grandchildren of Old Gnosticism aim at our disunity [**6**]
Why should we be the victims of intuition?

Believing in sin and the forbidden?
You, the nation-wide readers of my poems
Entrenched within graves:
Do not disbelieve in me,
I have no interest in my status
But mortgaged my impetuous moth to the forthcoming [7]
And piled tents on tents.

They hate the flowing river
The child's cry,
And sailing in the religion of love.
Ah, Abel's sister,
Write it down:
I am the one who recommends, [**8**]
And I am definitely the executor.
I shall die after death,
For the dead are already dead
And I am in conflict with death
I will die but I shall begin from my end. [**9**]

1. The title by this name Abel's Sister is the poet's creation. There is no reference to Abel's sister in the Holy Quran as such. According to the tale, Abel's sister was called Iqlima and was ugly but Cain's sister was called Luza and she was beautiful. Adam asked Abel to marry Loza which of course angered Cain and consequently, led to

his crime. In this context, Abel's sister may represent the image of a sympathetic , affectionate and motherly female.

2. May allude to the Quranic tale of the Companions of the Cave which resembles the legend of the Seven Sleepers in the Old Testament.

3. The Sumerian god of streams and water, Enki inhabited Delmon (the Bahrain islands). He is referred to as the Sumerian Noah because of his aim to save the humanity from the floods.

5. Direct reference to the futility of peace with Israel.

6. The term 'gnosis' is Greek and means wisdom; it refers here to a group of early Christians who believed they received direct enlightenment from God. They were considered heretics by the Church . However, Gnosticism paved the way for the rise of Sufism and mysticism in Islamic belief.

7. 'Impetuous moth' is a phrase mentioned in the Holy Quran to refer to the agitation and commotion of people during the Day of Judgment.

8. Ibrahim Shabaan together with Ali Al-Jalawi, constitute a new wave of politically committed poets in Bahraini contemporary poetry. Their poetry is exuberantly rich in imagery and allusions, in particular Quranic and Mesopotamian references. Often, the subjective personal tone prevails in their poetry, as is the case with this poem. However, subjectivity lies at the core of modern Arabic poetry; the proclaiming "I" is both the persona and the timeless aging voice of the past.

9. Noticeable in this poem is Ibrahim Shabaan's frequent use of interjections and refrains (which have been modified in the English version) and are meant for obvious emphatic purposes.

HUSAIN AL-SAMAHEEJI

Rituals

(The Climate of Love)

A distracted glance between us,
In a girdled controlled surrounding,
Chases me to the ashes of history.
Since I celebrated your eyes,
I had a homeland,
Spelling your beginning
On a portrait held between your two palms.
I removed from my heart what I inherited from Fire,
And blessed my soul in painting an eternal picture,
Certain of the flow of poetry on my lips
Certain of the choice of colour on my vigilant feather.
Among us never did the painful shore discard its revelation,
Among us the language is oppressed by guilt
So I ripped it off from my ribs.
Among us there is Fire
But with a subdued malice. [**1**]

(The Climate of Vision)

A homeland in the shape of cups,
Whose wine is your eyes,
And a body in its curves, intoxicating Time. [**2**]

Who will glance at the blushing moon in a party
In which the lover leans his face towards Heaven?

(The Climate of Writing)

All this wine poured on the body of paper
Is the season of our thrills.
All this escape from the stare,
Is a journey of wounds
Which hide in the mirrors our astonishments.
All this intoxicated blood
With traces of rhyme
Is sky pouring down its timings,
Which will form our destinations in a postal distance
Between the island and the scaffold.

An Iraqi Love Poem

Dozing between the two bosoms,
I dreamt like birds
Spreading and contracting their wings.
There was an Iraqi love poem in my pocket,
Muffled with grief and an incurable pain.
I tripped off my girl friend's bosoms
And laid on the bank of a river.
Intoxicated by a cup of ginger tea [**3**]
I began to waive to the passers-by.
The cup was swaying near me,

Calling for ecstasy in the deceitful dark,
Which lied between wakefulness and near death.
It stretched out and expanded:
There was poetry burning in its blood,
Softening my sadness with a dance near the river [**4**]
Scattering me in the skeleton of the poem.
I dozed again and again
Over the breast of a murdered person,
And began to look for a flower
In the flowing dunes.
I was a prophet searching for murderers in the trunks of the palm-trees,
Entertaining friends with stories about the cities
Which will prepare themselves for death the next day;
And cautioning the youths of the forthcoming devastation.
Ah, folks, I have seen what will be coming
So do not be afraid…
The soldiers will slumber on their alphabets
While the foreigners' shot at the cities
Will swing on the stairs.
Baghdad renounces outsiders,
Removes from its blood some wheat smell,
And the wind will be diverted from the south and the north.
Near the Tigris my girl-friend inures me to addiction;
She takes a puff whenever a word falls from my mouth,
Peels its skin from the body,
And it relaxes in its melody and the departure
Outside its narration of a country

Of which its children leave every day
And erect their tents for the remaining wounded
Who sleep on the fringe of sands.
Baghdad weeps on the brinks of fire
And I sip from her blood some wine,
And some of my blood clot in the veins of the clouds.
Some of my blood is not owed to a country,
It defies the prophets
Crucifies them
And scatter my smell in the remains of the poem. [**5**]

1. Husain Al-Samaheeji, uses the word 'fire' twice in this stanza. In both instances, it connotes passion and carnal desires.

2. It is very interesting to note that, though drinking wine is forbidden in Islam, reference to it is widely used among some Muslim poets. The tradition can be traced to the Persian poet Omar Al-Khayyam and his invigorating *Rubayiiat*. Here, Husain Al-Samaheeji's strong Shia leanings do not preclude him from drawing rather sensual images. Incidentally, sensual and erotic references can also be observed in Ibrahim Al-Arrayedh's poetry .

3. It has been a long tradition in Arab countries, perhaps based on some kind of psychological assumption, that tea, and especially black tea is a source of joyful stimulation. So the darker the tea is, the more 'kicks' a person will get. The 'intoxicated' should be understood in its non-literal meaning.

4. Husain Al-Samaheeji most probably refers to the shore on the river Tigris in Baghdad where the local restaurants and coffee shops used to be the most peaceful and exciting spots for both the tourists and the locals.

5. One of the promising voices in the contemporary Bahraini poetry, Husain Al-Samaheeji combines the rebellious spirit of the dwindling revolutionary past and the anger and the uneasiness of the younger generation of today in Bahrain. The fluidity of his images are skilfully woven within a narrative thread which adds excitement and at the same time sobriety to his poetry.

LAILA AL-SAYED

Four Lovers

(1)
Four
Lovers
Discovered the mirrors
Of God.
Firing on their hearts
They began the recordings of time
They brought a sapling rose
And a grip of light
And concealed honey in the lock of its hair [**1**]

(2)
Four lovers
Came
From the seasons of dream
Offering salt to the earth [**2**]

(3)
Suddenly
They traversed the sea conditions
And measured its temperature

(4)

Perhaps they taught the earth
Names
Full of joy

(5)

Fewer dense
Friends
Proffering the wave and the soul
An idea
Which followed Time
In its eternity

(6)

A pleasing tale
In a Sumerian river [**3**]
Ripped a cloud
Caused friends to alternate
In its celebration

(7)

He has a wisdom of birds [**4**]
But soon aged
In his professions

(8)
He ventured with her mirror
In a childhood risk
Turned then into
An acceptable villain!!

(9)
He came with some
Of her intuitions
She trembled
Like a moon
Like a wave
Carrying some of her blood

(10)
The friends' party
Ended in their loss [**5**]

We Passed There

(1)
We came back
Washing the passageways
With the lovers' voice
As he warmed up the darkness of the room.

(2)

We came back
For the first love
To make harbours from it
Which annoyed the sailors
Of its burial.

(3)

We came back
To the first sea
To extract from it
The locks of dream
To be unfolded
Before the Sun's face.

(4)

We came back
As ships
Followed by winter
Muttering the heart's sensation.

(5)

We came back
To the Heart's room
To confuse the passers-by
There.

(6)

I passed your shadow
Decoding the scripts of my letters.

(7)

Before the window
I passed a chair
With my slumbering body
Leaning on a smile.

(8)

Greetings of our shadows
Cross the plains
Chase our childhood
Draw small
Sullen locks
Before the camera.

(9)

Ah, Lord,
I shall leave the moon
Pass there
To write down
The sins
Of the little girl.

1. The image of honey should not be seen as bizarre for it is common in Arabic poetry and connotes beauty.

2. 'Salt' suggests sweetness and liveliness.

3. Referring to the ancient Sumerians who lived in the fertile lands in the Gulf and the present South Iraq between the Tigris and Euphrates.

4. A Quranic allusion referring to Al-Naml is found in chapter 17 of the Holy Quran where God endowed Prophet Solomon with a wisdom to speak the language of birds. On the other hand, the wisdom of birds (Manteq Al-Tayr) is the title of a book by the Persian mystic poet Sheikh Attar.

5. Noticeable in this poem is the manipulation of physical space within the structure of the poem. Laila Al-Sayed has grouped the words within a narrow spatial skeleton to produce a brilliant spatial communication. The poem is divided into ten stanzas, without any punctuation marks (except for two successive exclamation marks in stanza (8), each carrying not more than three words written on the right- hand side of the page. It is, therefore, not only the written script that communicates with the readers but also the massive white space that sings an unheard song. Laila Al-Sayed's poetry, in general, is characterized by brevity, its visual quality and touches of feminine sensuality.

PARWEEN HABIB

Blood-stained Light [1]

I

I behold you in the lovers' corners,
At the moment of the budding of violets,
To the surprise of the villages,
An absent homeland. [**2**]

Days of benevolence and love
And our destiny
As we recall our childhood.

Arise then,
So we can give birth to a blood-stained Time.
There, they kindle the gate of apprehensions,
Reside in the eve of the hearts
And purchase with our clamour the kingdom of imagination.

II

You are the plain on which
A deserted youth steps;
In your brush, lie a willow,
A light and a blade.
You are a river

Carried by a secret in the dawn
Like a thrill amongst passions.
Like a crying cloud passing the bed
And wrapped in slumbers.

III

With your brush
Often you walked out stealthily,
Whilst the moon snatched your prayers,
But reappeared after a long concealment.

My beloved,
The city would not survive
Whilst you were there making a doll's forehead…
Ah, Man of Void…
Who are you?
A time you are confined in the groans of the learned,
Who left
Behind their footsteps
In
The tears
Of the fences.
And times you come to us;
We, who are abducted to the drizzle of graves by Jasmine.

It Elevates Me to Fullness

Infinitely,
Your love
Was
Escorting me
Every evening
From the coffeepot and other things
High
To the seclusion of the priests and the dwelling of the nymphs.
Whilst I was carrying the frowning of women
And the anxiety of the slow night:
You said to me: pour down
And we almost fell on a cloud,
As though my heart was heeding the day's confusions,
And the chaos of ascension.
And whilst I hastened to follow the clinging of the summit,
Leaving behind my anger
In the crooked bed and passion replete with the body's rain,
I pulled you towards my lips. [**3**]

1.To appreciate Parween Habib's poetry one has to plunge deep into the erotic imageries of the Syrian Nezar Qabbani's poetry. Redolent with amatory images, Qabbani's steadfast addressee, like the mistress of English courtier poets, is often absent. Interestingly enough, Parween Habib's persona in her poetry presents her response to Qabbani's infatuations.

2. 'Homeland' is a recurrent theme in the poetry of most contemporary poets in Bahrain. Sometimes it transcends the physical reality and other times as in the case of

Parween Habib is pinned in the unconscious where its absence denotes its presence. It may also refer to Parween Habib's sense of alienation and estrangement by living outside the homeland.

3. Parween Habib's love poems reflect the torture of the soul rather than the body. There is a mystical strain in her approach, it is not the infatuation or possession of the physical love that she seeks; rather, the Absolute love, the infinite and the unadulterated.

AHMAD AL-SITRAWI

A Prayer

Still waiting for return,
For the past kiss
Where lies between his lips
The pain of letters.
Will the mellowed silence enter?

A Female

I shall proceed,
Perhaps the distance will shorten.
Still I am ignorant of all the twists,
And my lady still is an orphan,
Waiting for my presence
Here.

Wait for me as an orphan;
I am familiar with the orphans,
Though they ignore me.
So if we are not all accommodated,
The night will embrace us
Even if all those present vanished.

Hasan Marhamah

The Field of Silence

And for Silence there is a field,
Descended from me,
Because the snow
Which is gathered
Is murdered in speech.
There is a window for the wound,
Peeled off from its salt,
And it rises on a world of ashes and vaults,
Where the innocent pus is removed,
And the wound is born
Out of coalescence.
I endeavour
discontentedly
Therefore, I start on a non-distant travel
Through the cities.
This intermingling worries me,
And the longing for a yellow paper
Buried by minutes,
Horrifies me
I inhabited the sky,
Befriended the stars,
And crossed to the selected point
But there is a lock on the earth,
Oh, you, the Clothed One [**1**]
Between Heaven and me
Will you descend here

And then depart ?

I am a language
Whose letters have been confiscated
As a fall
In search of a place to collide.

1. A Quranic allusion referring to Al-Mudather Sura (The Clothed One) in which God addresses the Prophet as founder of the most Benevolent Order.

ALI AL-JALAWI*

A Man in a Mistaken Era

It seems that the masters have been disappointed by our Age so they kept withdrawing one by one

In Damascus, I saw you among the nymphs:
An Arab boy,
Who was clearing his sorrow
On its stony walls on a wintry night.

Dewdrops slumbered in his palms,
In a capital oblivious of its orphanhood,
And the song vanished in the alley of speech.

I saw you descending from Dhuffar; [**1**]
The train was postponed until the next run,
Over your sanctioned blood dozed Heaven.

I saw you a prophet in the concealed language,
Unashamed of your wound.
I saw you,
When you patted on the top of my country's palm-tree,
I saw you in every face,
And Damascus which now has realized your grief,

Looked smaller than it was.

Ah, the last prophet,
Damascus is back,
And your body teaches us self-esteem,
Ah, the last guardian,
We deserted you to be drowned alone,
Though we came back.
Our apology to you
As if we were devastated by Karbala. [**2**]

I saw you in a mistaken era,
In a confined era,
Hardly in accord with your stature,
The era, which of despair,
The great masters left behind.

And Damascus will be back
To its orphanhood,
Like a child resigning to his broken game,
To plunge his dreams into a cry.

Ah, the last of the nobles,
I saw you on the terrace,
The road led to your free blood,
I saw you how you traversed time
To the land of martyrs.

Hasan Marhamah

*Ali Al-Jalawi is the offspring of the younger generation of Bahraini poets with a strong Islamist outlook. Imprisoned twice at an early age, Al-Jalawi exhibits in his poems the sufferings of the Shia community in remarkable poetic images often fused with Quranic allusions and philosophical undertones. His voice is as revolutionary and prophetic as that of the Marxist poets of the sixties and seventies.

1. A province in present Oman

2 .Karbala is the name of the battle in which the fourth Shia Imam Husain Bin Ali fought the tyrant Yazid Bin Muaweiah, of the Umayyad dynasty on the tenth of Muharram 61 of the Hegira Era (HE), (9 October 61 of Christian Era (CE). Imam Husain, together with 72 of his followers, were brutally murdered by Yazid's huge army and members of his family were taken captive. Ali Al-Jalawi has skilfully woven the event of Karbala and the murder of Husain Bin Ali and his followers into this poem by using images related to blood, martyrdom, orphanhood, and betrayal.

SAWSAN DAHNEEM

Deaf Echoes

Whenever I was assured that you lied in heart,
I would demolish the alphabets
And would share my silence with throbbing
So to be more mindful of departure…
The pomegranate that you could not hold in your hands,
Will be split in front of your lips,
And will reveal your laughter as you tear it by your sharp teeth
To stimulate you with its piety…!! [**1**]

The child whom you hurdled her way once…
Could not be purified unless you trailed your reductive sins: love and blood…
Distance rose naked from its madness,
Stole the confession…
And enjoyed its miles whenever flirted with by desire…
Does distance realize that yearning has restless masts
As waves possessing eyes that appeal to the blind?
It is the wind that blows away our steps as the time of reunion arrives;
It is the soul that gathers steps
To run away with fugitives
But of a love!
Cain never had a moment of love, [**2**]

Committed the sinful act

And in the flame of retribution he fell.

Hence paradise was set on fire.

Let passion openly scorch the legislators' bodies,

For they ask the Lord for the flower of Salvation,

To enrich their hearts with the dream of summer

For it was God who planted the pulse in the sanctuary of the Virgin Mary [**3**]

So a prophet should be born.

But the clouds were about to share his rain

For that woman had reflections of the Queen of Sheba; [**4**]

The more she was inflamed in caution

In scent Solomon rekindled her… [**5**]

1. What makes Sawsan Dahneem's poems obscure and rather unintelligible is the fact that she resorts to discordant and far-fetched imageries which are impregnated with allusions and inept punctuation marks as shown in the above poem.

2. Refers to the story of Cain and his brother Abel. Because God accepted Abel's sacrifice and rejected Cain's, jealousy and greed drove Cain to murder his brother while he was asleep under the tree. Eventually, he died of his malicious act and that was his punishment.

3. The Virgin Mary is the only woman whose name is explicitly mentioned in the Holy Quran and a whole Sura is devoted to her family and life. The allusion here is to the impregnation of the Virgin Mary by God's Spirit and consequently the birth of Jesus Christ as referred to in the Holy Quran and also the doubts and skepticism of her own people until the baby Christ revealed her innocence.

4. In Arabic and Islamic books she is referred to as 'Balqees'. Her story is mentioned in the Holy Quran together with the prophet Solomon. The allusion here is to her wisdom and discretion for accepting Solomon's invitation to worship God instead of

the stars. At first, she was cautious of his intentions, but later she moved towards him treading on a carpet of mirrors and eventually she realized that he was propagating the word of God and, therefore, embraced the new religion. 'Balqees' is also the title of the longest poem by the Syrian poet Nezar Qabbani dedicated to his wife Balqees who was killed in a bomb blast in Lebanon in 1982.

5. The story of the Prophet Solomon is mentioned in the Holy Quran. He was endowed with the skill of communication with the birds. He was informed by the bird hoopoe that the Queen of Sheba (Balqees) and her people worshiped the sun and other stars so he sent a proclamation to her inviting her to worship God. After her conversion, Solomon married her.

Biographical Notes (in alphabetical order)

AHMAD AL-AJAMI (1958-)

Born in the village of Al-Deraz, Bahrain. Completed his primary education at schools in Bahrain. Joined Kuwait University, but for some political reasons was unable to continue his studies. His first collection was entitled: *She is Plain, She a Vision*, 1987. It was followed by *The Off-spring of Lamps*, 1990, *The Scarlet Rituals*, 1993, *The Rose of Fear*, 1999, *A Lover*, 1997, *Perhaps it's Me*, 1999, & *An Evening in My Hand*, 2003. He is member of the Bahrain Writers' Society

FATHIYA AL-AJLAN (1953-)

Born in the city of Al-Muharraq, Bahrain. Completed her education at schools in Bahrain. Her collections include: *The Midday Sun,* 1983 (colloquial poetry co-written with the poet Ali Al-Sharqawi), *The Mast of Love*, 1984, *As I came, My Blood Fled*, 1988, *The Sins of the Wind* (colloquial) 1999, *The Margins of a Marginalized Woman*, 1998.

IBRAHIM AL-ARRAYEDH (1908-2001)

Born in the city of Mumbai, India. His mother died when he was young and thus he was brought up by an Indian governess. Al-Arrayedh completed his schooling in India and came home to work as English language teacher in 1925. He was taught the Arabic language and Arabic literature by the poet, Salman Al-Tajer. His first collection *Remembrance* was published in 1931, *Wa Mutasam* (poetic play) in 1931, *Brides* in 1946, *Two Kisses* (ballad) in 1946, *The Land of Martyrs* (epic) in 1951, *Candles,* 1965, *Khayyam Quartets* (translation) in 1935, and he published other miscellaneous poems. Al-Arrayedh also held several positions: Speaker of the Constitutional Parliament in 1973, and Ambassador-at- Large in 1975 until his death in 2001.

ALAWI AL-HASHMI (1946-)

Born in the city of Manamah, Bahrain. He completed his primary and secondary education at schools in Bahrain. He received his BA from the Arab Beirut University in 1972, his MA from Cairo University in 1978 and his Ph.D. from Tunisia in 1986. His first collection *Sparrows and the Shadow of a Tree* was published in 1977. He published *Where Does Grief Come From?* in 1980 and *Stations for Hardship* in 1988. He also produced some outstanding critical studies on Arabic Poetry: *What Has the Palm-tree Said to the Sea: A Critical Study of Contemporary Poetry in Bahrain* in 1981, *Contemporary Poets of Bahrain* in 1988, *Critical Readings of Ali Sharqawi's New Solos of Dhahi Bin Waleed,* 1989, *The Mobile Consonant* in three parts, 1992, 1993 & 1995; *The Phenomenon of Hypertextuality in Modern Saudi Poetry*, 1998 & *The Philosophy of Rhythm in Arabic Poetry* in 2006.

Dr. Alwai Al-Hashmi worked at the University of Bahrain as the Professor of Modern Arabic Literature until his appointment as Director of Higher Education in Bahrain Ministry of Education in 2007.

SALMAN AL-HAYKI (1952-)

Born in Manamah, Bahrain. Received his B.Ed in 1970 and BA in Arabic Language & Literature in 1974. His first volume, *Predators*, was published in 1991, followed by *Rabab Hia Al-Batool*, 1992, *Rain on the Face of My Beloved*, 1993, *The Sobs of the Planet*, 1998, *Rainbow* (poetic play), 2000. He is member of the Bahrain Writers' Society and currently works as journalist at the Al-Akhbar Al-Khaleej Newspaper.

ALI AL-JALAWI (1975-)

Born in the city of Manamah. His first volume, *Two faces of One Woman* was published in 1999, followed by *Disobedience* in 2000, *The Last City* in 2002, *The Delmon Cycle* I in 2002, *The Delmon Cycle II* in 2003. Homepage: http://www.jallawi.org/

JAFFAR AL-JAMRI (1961-)

Born in the village of Beni Jamrah , Bahrain. Completed his education at schools in Bahrain. He is member of the UAE Writers' union and the Union of Arab Writers. His first volume *The Geography of Paradise* was published in 1988, and *Something Distracting my Lung* in 1992. He is the editor of Poetry and Culture section at Al-Wasat Newspaper.

AHMAD MOHAMMAD AL-KHALIFA (1929- 2004)

Born in the village of Al-Jassrah, Bahrain. He moved later to Zallaq village when he was three years old. He lived in Zallaq and grew up amongst its gardens and vales. In 1951 and at the age of 23, Ahmad AlKhalifa moved to the Al-Gudaybiya district in Manamah where he began his early literary career. His first collection *Songs from Bahrain* was published in 1955; *Heat and Mirage* followed in 1962; *The Remains of Treachery* in 1966; *The Moon and the Palm-Tree* in 1978, *Clouds in the Summer* in 1988, *What Bahrain Said to Kuwait* in 1991.

YOQOOB AL-MUHARRAQI (1950-)

Born in Bahrain. After completing his early schooling, Al-Muharraqi traveled to France to study the art of cinema production and eventually settled in Qatar and then moved to the UAE. Al-Muharraqi published his first collection of poems in 1973, entitled *The Sufferings of Ahmad Bin Al-Majid* together with other miscellaneous poems.

ABDUL HAMID AL-QAED (1947-)

Born in Manamah, Bahrain. First, he worked in a local bank but later established an independent Translation House. He is member of the Bahrain Writers' Society. Translated various essays and literary texts from English into Arabic. His first collection entitled *A Lover in the Season of Thirst* was published in 1975, followed by *Noise of Whisper* in 2003, *Alienation of Violets* in 2009, and *The Anthology of Modern Bahraini Poetry* in 2009.

SAEED AL-OWEINATI (1950-1976)

Born in the village of Al-Khamis, Bahrain. Completed his university studies in Iraq. Worked as an editor at Al-Mawaqaf magazine until his death in 1976. His first volume *To You My Beloved, To You My Homeland* was published in 1976.

AHMAD AL-SITRAWI (1972-)

Born in the city of Muharraq, Bahrain. He is member of the Bahrain Writers' Society. His first volume, *I am not a Prophet* (n.d.), followed by *A Female* (n.d.), *A Prayer* (n.d.) , *A Shade Over a Dozing Shade* (n.d.), *Khdyja* (n.d.), *Time-Bound Shirt* in 2007, *The Forgotten King* (poetic play) (n.d.) , & *The Biography of Body* (novel) (n.d.).

LAILA AL-SAYED (1967-)

Born in Bahrain. Received her BA in Arabic Language & Literature in 1992. She published in both standard and colloquial Gulf Arabic. Her first collection was *We Passed There* in 2003, *Who Inherits my Smile* (Translated from Arabic) in 2005, *The Taste of Isolation* 2006, *My ink-stained Palm* 2007, *I Knock on the Sea Doors to Enter the Gazelle Tower* in 2008. Presently, she works as a senior Teacher of the Arabic Language in Bahrain.

HUSAIN AL-SAMAHEEJI (1967-)

Born in the village of Samaheej, Bahrain. Received his BA & MA in Arabic Literature. His first volume of poetry *What Never Said by Abu Taher Al-Qurmati*, was published in 1996, followed by *Crows*, 1999, *Another Woman*, 1999, *Oriental Whims* in 2002. He has also published miscellaneous critical studies.

AHMAD AL-SHAMLAN (1942-)

Born in the district of Umul- Hassam in Manamah, Bahrain. He completed his higher education in the former USSR. Al-Shamlan began writing at an early age. His first collection *Lilies of Love* was published in 1987, *The Remains of Green* followed in 1989, *Barbaar Queen* (poetic play) in 1994, *A Smell in the Memory* in 1998, *Annihilation and Writing* (criticism) in 1999, *The Bells of Hope* (criticism) in 2001 and Miscellaneous critical essays.

FAWZIA AL-SINDI (1957-)

Born in the city of Manamah, Bahrain. Completed her graduate studies in Egypt in the field of Business. Her first volume *Awakening* was published in 1984, *Do I see around me, Do I describe what Happened* in 1986. This was followed by *The Absent Man's Throat* in 1992, *The Last Windward* in 1998, *The Soul's Refuge* in 1999, and *The Hostage of Pain* in 2005.

IMAN ASSIRI (1952-)

Born in the city of Manamah. Graduated from Teachers College and worked as teacher in Bahrain schools. Her first collection entitled *It's Me a Skylark* was published in 1982, followed by *Five Minutes for My Heart*, 1996, *Timely Conversation with the Skylark* in 2001, *The Skylark's Small Secrets* in 2004, *A Female's Book* in 2005, and *Desires* in 2009.

IBRAHIM BU-HINDI (1948-)

Born in the city of Manamah, Bahrain. Received his Masters in Business Administration from Sheffield University, England. Bu-Hindi wrote in both standard and colloquial Gulf Arabic. His first collection *Dreams of the Twilight Star* (colloquial) was published in 1974; *Disobedient Time* (play) in 1974, *Suroor* (play) in 1975; *Testimony of Love* in 1987; *Does Heart Dry Up* (play) in 1987; *Courtship of Quarry* in 1994; *A Combat* in 1994 and *The Rise of the Slaughtered Man* in 2006. Bu Hindi chaired the Bahrain Writers' Society from 2004 until 2009.

SAWSAN DAHNEEM (1980-)

Born in Bahrain. Graduated from Bahrain University, College of Business Administration. Her first collection, *Absent, But* was published

1998; *A Kiss in the Windward of Forgetfulness* in 2001; *He Built His Throne on the Water* in 2008. Presently, she works as journalist at Al-Methaq Newspaper.

PARWEEN HABIB (1969-)

Born in the city of Manamah, Bahrain. Received her BA in Arabic Language & Literature in 1993, MA in 1997, and Ph.D. in 2008. Her critical study of the poetry of the Syrian poet, Nezar Qabbani, entitled *Technicalities of Composition in the Poetry of Nezar Qabbani,* was published in 1999. Her first volume of poetry *Your Scared Manhood and My Paper-like Childhood* was published in 2001. Presently, she works as TV presenter in the UAE.

QASIM HADDAD (1948-)

Born in the city of Al-Muharraq, Bahrain. He was educated in schools in Bahrain but for political and social reasons he did not continue his study. Qasim Haddad is one of the founders of the Bahrain Writers' Society where he had several leading posts. His first collection entitled *Portents* was published in 1970; *Love's Heart*, 1970; *The Exit of the Martyr's Head from the Treasonous City*,1972; *The Second Blood*, 1975; *Judgment Day*, 1980; *Splinters*, 1981; *Inclinations*, 1982; *Al-Nahrawan* 1988; *Armour* (with the novelist Amin Saleh), 1989; *Escorted with Mountain Goats*, 1990; *The Isolation of Queens*, 1992; *Criticism of Hope*, 1995; *Majnoon Laila*, 1996; *Qasim's Tomb*, 1997; *Not This Way, Not That Way*, 1997; *Distance Therapy*, 2000; *Not A Guest Anymore*, 2007. Homepage: http://www.qhaddad.com

YOUSIF HASAN (1942-)

Born in the village of Daih, in Manamah, Bahrain to a conservative family. He completed his primary education and then joined the Bahrain Petroleum Company. In 1978 he received his BA in Arabic Language & Literature from the Arab Beirut University. His first collection was entitled *The Village Songs* published in 1988.

ALI ABDULLA KHALIFA (1944-)

Born in the city of Al-Muharraq , Bahrain to a family of pearl-divers. He completed his education at schools in Bahrain and then joined the Directorate of Customs. His first collection entitled *Moans of the Dhow Masts* published in 1965; *The Thirst of Palm-Trees* followed in 1966, *An Illumination on the Memory of the Homeland* in 1973; *Clover Buds* in 1981; *In the Farewell of the Green Lady* in 1992. Ali Abdulla Khalifa also wrote in colloquial Gulf Arabic and his collection entitled *Evening Sparrows* was published in 1983.

HAMDAH KHAMIS (1946-)

Born in Bahrain. She completed her early education in Bahrain and travelled to Iraq and Morocco for her higher education. However, she came back without continuing her higher education to work as teacher in Bahrain. Her first collection entitled *Apology to Childhood* was published in 1978; and her second collection *Hymns* in 1985.

AHMAD MADAN (1955-)

Born in the village of Al-Noweidrat, Bahrain. Completed his graduate study in the filed of architecture at Riyadh University in 1980. He is a member of the Bahrain Writers' Society. His first volume, *The Morning of Writing* was published in 1984, followed by *Grass for the Blood of Paper* in 1992.

HASAN MARHAMAH (1949-)

Born in the city of Manamah, Bahrain. Completed his early schooling in Bahrain. Received his BA (English) from Riyadh University (Saudi Arabia) in 1974, MA from Bangalore University, (India) in 1976. In 1979 he joined the University of Wales, where he completed his M.Ed. in 1981 and PhD in 1985. Upon his return from the UK, he was appointed Assistant Professor of Modern English literature at the University of Bahrain. In 1994 he was promoted to the rank of Associate Professor and became Chairman of the English Department in 1996, then the Department of Foreign Languages in 1999, and Project

Director of the College of Community Service in 2001. In 2004 he resigned from the University of Bahrain. He has written extensively on both literary as well as educational topics. He has three more books under publication: *A Glossary of Contemporary Literary Terms* (Arabic-English), *The Poetry of the Priest-poet, Ronald Stuart Thomas* (in Arabic) and *She Who Brought Rock Flowers to Uruk* (novel).

ABDUL RAHMAN MOHAMMAD RAFI (1936-)

Born in the city of Manamah, Bahrain. He had his early education at schools in Bahrain. Abdul Rahman Rafi is eloquent in both standard and colloquial Gulf Arabic. His first collection in standard Arabic is Songs *of the Four Seas* published in 1970; *Rotation on the Distance* followed in 1979; *He Asks Me* in 1981, and three volumes in colloquial Gulf Arabic which were collected in one book entitled *Anthology of Colloquial Poetry* and published in 1980.

KARIM REDHI (1960-)

Born in the village of Tubli, Bahrain. Graduated from Technical school in 1979. He worked in the Bahrain Ministry of Water & Electricity and Petroleum Company in the UAE. He is member of the Bahrain Writers' Society. His first critical work, (co-written with other writers), was entitled *A Text in the Forest of Interpretation* and published in 2000; *Classroom Chats*, a collection of poems in 2003.

ALI Al-SHARQAWI (1948-)

Born in the city of Manamah, Bahrain. After completing his secondary education, Al-Sharqawi spent two years in Iraq but came back to work in the Ministry of Health. His poetry career began at an early age. He published his first collection entitled: *Thunder in the season of Draught* in 1975; *The Heart's Palm-Tree* in 1981; *The New Solo of Dhai Bin Waleed* in 1982; *She is the Thought and Possibility* in 1983; *A Vision of Victory* in 1983; *Vocations of little Sea-gulls* in 1987; *Memories of Hearth* in 1988; *Wa Aarabaa* in 1991; *The Crimson Dining-Table* in 1994; *The Manuscripts of Geith Bin Al-Bera'a* in 1995, *The Ibex* in 1998; *The Book of Disgrace* in 1998; *Ibn Haweya's Papers* in 2001, *Sparrows' Songs* (a collection of poems for children) in 1983, *Key to Happiness* (poetic play) in 1984.

IBRAHIM SHABAAN (1963-)

Born in Bahrain. Received his BA in Arabic Language & Literature. He published his first collection, *My Destiny* in 1991, *A Woman refuses Peace* followed in 1993, *Farewell to Eve* in 1994, *With Love to the Homeland* in 1994, *One Heart One Love* in 1997, *Love Not Reproach* in 1997, *Trembling with Heart* in 2000, and *Dawn of Speech* in 2001.

FATIMA TAITOON (1962-)

Born in the city of Manamah, Bahrain. Received her BA from Kuwait University in 1982 in Arabic Language & Literature. She published her first collection, *I Draw My Heart*, in 1991 followed by *Deserted Times* in 1994, *Love Rituals* in 1996, *A White Man* in 1996, *My Beloved Who* in 1998, & *He is in Silence Forever* in 2008. Presently, she works as journalist in Al-Ayam Newspaper.

NABEELA ZUBARI (1954-)

Born in Bahrain. Received her MA from the University of Wales and Ph.D. in Educational Technology from Leeds University, England. Her first collection, *Grey Obstacles* was published in 1994, *Wish the Sea Come Back* in 1998, *Blue Whisper* in 2006 and *A Pulse on my Papers* in 2008.

Presently, she works as the Professor of Educational Technology at the University of Bahrain.